Rigor in Your School:
A Toolkit for Leaders

Ronald Williamson
and
Barbara R. Blackburn

EYE ON EDUCATION

EYE ON EDUCATION
6 DEPOT WAYWEST, SUITE 106
LARCHMONT, NY 10538
(914) 833–0551
(914) 833–0761 fax
www.eyeoneducation.com

Library of Congress Cataloging-in-Publication Data

Williamson, Ronald D.
  Rigor in your school : a toolkit for leaders / Ronald Williamson and Barbara R.
Blackburn.
    p. cm.
  Includes bibliographical references.
  ISBN 978-1-59667-176-8
  1. School improvement programs. 2. Educational leadership. I. Blackburn, Bar-
bara R., 1961- II. Title.
  LB2822.8.W556 2011
  371.2'07--dc22

                                                          2010048396

10 9 8 7 6 5 4 3 2

Production services provided by
Rick Soldin a Book/Print Production Specialist
www.book-comp.com

Also Available from Eye On Education

Rigorous Schools and Classrooms: Leading the Way
Ronald Williamson and Barbara R. Blackburn

Rigor Is Not a Four-Letter Word
Barbara R. Blackburn

The Principalship from A to Z
Ronald Williamson and Barbara R. Blackburn

Study Guide: The Principalship from A to Z
Ronald Williamson and Barbara R. Blackburn

Classroom Motivation from A to Z:
How to Engage Your Students in Learning
Barbara R. Blackburn

Study Guide: Classroom Motivation from A to Z
Barbara R. Blackburn

Classroom Instruction from A to Z:
How to Promote Student Learning
Barbara R. Blackburn

Study Guide: Classroom Instruction from A to Z
Barbara R. Blackburn

Classroom Walkthroughs to Improve Teaching and Learning
Donald S. Kachur, Judith A. Stout, and Claudia L. Edwards

Motivating and Inspiring Teachers, 2nd Edition:
The Educational Leader's Guide for Building Staff Morale
Todd Whitaker, Beth Whitaker, and Dale Lumpa

Get Organized!
Time Management for School Leaders
Frank Buck

Executive Skills for Busy School Leaders
Christopher Hitch and Dave Coley

What Great Principals Do *Differently*:
15 Things That Matter Most
Todd Whitaker

We dedicate this book to those who work everyday to increase rigor so their students will be better prepared for the future.

I dedicate this book to my mother, Josephine, who always modeled a strong work ethic and a lifelong iniquisitiveness. Her dedication to family and faith shapes my life every day. You are missed.

Ron

I dedicate this book to my son, Hunter, whose 13-year-old perspective on school and teachers helps me focus on what is most important.

Barbara

Acknowledgments

We'd like to thank the following people who supported our work:

♦ Our families and friends for their encouragement and patience as we worked to meet deadlines.

♦ Bob Sickles for his regular feedback and advice.

♦ Robert Blackburn for his expertise and support on advocacy.

♦ Toni Eubank, Director of Making Middle Grades Work, Southern Regional Education Board, for her description of the Instant Credit Recovery option in Chapter Eight and for her in-depth response to a concern that allowing students to redo work does not prepare them for real life. Her insight added to our perspective.

♦ Colleagues in the Department of Leadership and Counseling at Eastern Michigan University.

♦ The principals and teachers throughout the country who talked with us about their schools and their efforts to improve rigor. We appreciate the work you do, as well as the ideas that made this book more useful.

♦ *The Principals' Partnership*; Pasadena Independent School District, Texas; and Chicago Area Three, who provided feedback and examples throughout this process.

♦ The thoughtful reviewers who read early drafts and offered helpful suggestions: Carolyn Guthrie, Miami-Dade County Schools, FL; Karen Hickman, Pasadena Independent School District, TX; Janet Hurt, Logan County School District, KY; and Ann Linson, East Noble School Corporation, IN.

♦ Dave Strauss, whose creativity always results in an inviting cover for our books.

♦ Lauren Beebe, who "went the extra mile" facilitating the book production process.

Meet the Authors

Ronald Williamson is a professor of educational leadership at Eastern Michigan University. Previously he taught at the University of North Carolina at Greensboro and was a teacher, principal, and executive director of instruction at the Ann Arbor, Michigan public schools.

Ron also served as executive director of the National Middle School Association, as a member of Middle Level Council of the National Association of Secondary School Principals, and as president of the National Forum to Accelerate Middle Grades Reform. He received the Gruhn-Long-Melton Award from NASSP in recognition of lifetime achievement in secondary school leadership, the Teaching Excellence Award from the University of North Carolina at Greensboro, and the Alumni Teaching Excellence Award from Eastern Michigan University.

The author of more than 100 books, chapters, papers, and articles in all the major professional journals serving middle and high school teachers and administrators, Ron works with schools throughout the country on school improvement projects.

Ron provided direct service to several large urban districts when he was selected by the Edna McConnell Clark Foundation to be a leadership coach in its national school reform project. He also worked with the Galef Institute in Los Angeles on a Comprehensive School Reform project to improve schools in New York City, Louisville, Houston, and Los Angeles. Currently, Ron is the content editor and editor of Research Briefs for *The Principals Partnership* website, sponsored by the Union Pacific Foundation. He also provides technical assistance and serves as the evaluator of *The Principals' Leadership Program*, an Oregon GEAR UP project.

Ron works regularly with schools and leadership teams on some of the following topics:

- Planning a Rigorous School

- Instructional Leadership Tools

- Managing Resistant Teachers

- Leadership Coaching and Development

- Structures to Support a Rigorous School

- Assessing Rigor in Schools

- Developing School Improvement Plans Focused on Rigor

- Improving the Work of Leadership Teams

If you'd like information about Ron and his work, contact him through his website: www.ronwilliamson.com.

Barbara R. Blackburn has dedicated her life to raising the level of rigor and motivation for professional educators and students alike. What differentiates Barbara's books are her easily executable concrete examples based on decades of experience as a teacher, professor, and consultant. Barbara's dedication to education was inspired in her early years by her parents, Bob and Rose. Her father's doctorate and lifetime career as a professor taught her the importance of professional training. Her mother's career as school secretary shaped Barbara's appreciation of the effort all staff play in the education of every child.

Barbara has taught early childhood, elementary, middle, and high school students and has served as an educational consultant for three publishing companies. She holds a master's degree in school administration and is certified as a school principal in North Carolina. She received her Ph.D. in Curriculum and Teaching from the University of North Carolina at Greensboro. In 2006, she received the award for Outstanding Junior Professor at Winthrop University. She recently left her position at the University of North Carolina at Charlotte to write and speak full-time.

In addition to speaking at state and national conferences, she also regularly presents workshops for teachers and administrators in elementary, middle, and high schools. Her workshops are lively and engaging and filled with practical information. Her most popular topics include:

- Rigor is NOT a Four Letter Word

- Rigorous Schools and Classrooms: Leading the Way

- Instructional Strategies that Motivate Students

- Content Literacy Strategies for the Young and the Restless

- Motivating Yourself and Others

- Engaging Instruction Leads to Higher Achievement

- High Expectations and Increased Support Lead to Success

- For more information, please contact her at her website: www.barbarablackburnonline.com.

If you would like to arrange on-site presentations, video chats, book study groups, or other professional services from Ronald Williamson and/or Barbara Blackburn, please contact Eye On Education at (888) 299-5350 or www.eyeoneducation.com.

Contents

4 Ownership and Shared Vision 51

5 Managing Data 67

Free Downloads

Many of the tools discussed and displayed in this book are also available on Eye On Education's website as Adobe Acrobat files. Permission has been granted to purchasers of this book to download these tools and print them.

You can access these downloads by visiting Eye On Education's website: www.eyeon-education.com. From the home page, click on FREE Downloads or search or browse our website to find this book. Scroll down for downloading instructions.

Your book-buyer access code is **RYS-7176-8**.

List of Free Downloads

Introduction

Rigor in Your School: A Toolkit for Leaders is third in our series of books on rigor. Barbara's book, *Rigor is NOT a Four-Letter Word*, was written specifically for teachers and is filled with classroom-based activities for all grade levels and subject areas. *Rigorous Schools and Classrooms: Leading the Way*, the second book, was written for principals and other leaders who sought school-wide strategies to increase rigor. During our work with schools, we were asked for even more examples of tools that could be used to promote rigor. *Rigor in Your School: A Toolkit for Leaders* is the result of those inquiries.

If you've read *Rigorous Schools and Classrooms*, you'll note how this text parallels that one, providing additional tools and more depth. If you haven't read *Rigorous Schools and Classrooms*, this book stands alone as a guidebook to leading your school to higher levels of rigor.

Chapter One provides an overview of the entire book, as well as a guide to the tools in each chapter. In Chapter Two, we present a clear definition of rigor, resources for related research, and an overview of our BASE Planning model. Chapters Three through Nine describe tools for each area of our COMPASS model: Culture, Ownership and Shared Vision, Managing Data, Professional Development, Advocacy, Shared Accountability, and Structures to Support Success. These chapters are not sequential; you may start with any area that interests you.

Our focus in this book is simple: to provide all school leaders with tools to improve rigor. We view leadership through a comprehensive lens—all those who currently hold a leadership position, those who aspire to a leadership role, and those who are leaders, even if they do not have a designated title. Just as principals will find some tools applicable to their role, a teacher-leader involved in curriculum revision will find useful tools. We include a variety of tools in each chapter so you may choose the ones that work best for your situation.

Choose is a key word. We are continually asked, "Which tool is best?" Our answer is always, "It depends." Often, a tool that works well in one school may be less effective in another. Always consider your situation, goals, and personnel to choose the tool or tools that will work for you. And remember, if one tool doesn't give you the results you want, consider using another.

The chapters in this book follow a consistent format. You'll find a short introduction to the topic, then a listing of all the chapter tools at the beginning of each chapter. We'll always give you appropriate contextual information, followed by the description of the tool. Many of the tools are formatted so that you may duplicate them, and electronic versions of some tools are available as Free Downloads from www.eyeoneducation.com.

One feature of this book is the inclusion of a series of "What if..." boxes. As we've worked with schools, we have been asked many questions. We've taken some of the most frequently asked questions and developed answers that you could use to respond to them when they arise. We hope you find our responses helpful as you work to overcome obstacles to your efforts to improve rigor in your school.

We believe strongly in providing every student with access to rigorous learning and know that courageous principals and skillful teachers are the key to making that a reality. Hopefully, these tools will be helpful as you work together to improve your school. We'd love to hear from you. Please visit our website, www.rigorineducation.com to contact us.

1

Leadership for Increased Rigor

Throughout this book we'll provide a clear, understandable definition of rigor, and discuss its impact on curriculum, instruction, and assessment. Although we believe that real instructional change, including increasing rigor, begins at the classroom level, we also believe school-wide efforts create the climate supportive of these changes. We've worked with principals, district leaders, and teachers for more than twenty years. The most successful schools are those that recognize that change is a constant, that improvement is a journey, not an event.

In Chapter One, we will preview each chapter of the book, as well as detail the tools included in each chapter. Then, we'll turn our attention to some of the assumptions you may hold. Finally, we'll ask you to reflect on your current vision for your school or district, which you will use as a basis for a later activity.

Tools in Chapter One: Rigor, Research, and the Change Model	
Tool 1	Check Your Own Assumptions
Tool 2	Your Personal Vision

In Chapter Two, we will present our definition of rigor, resources for related research, and an overview of our BASE Planning model. This chapter will provide you a concise foundation of information as you move forward.

Tools in Chapter Two: Rigor, Research, and the Change Model	
Tool 3	Rubric Reflections
Tool 4	Assessing Where You Are Now
Tool 5	Digging Deeper Into Research
Tool 6	Begin Your Planning
Tool 7	Implementation Planning Activities
Tool 8	Planning Activities for Sustaining Success
Tool 9	Evaluating and Adjusting Your Plan

The journey to becoming a more rigorous school is not straight, but winding. To successfully navigate the road it is important to take along a good set of tools: a road map, useful contact information, and a GPS unit or compass. This toolkit will provide you with a set of tools in the form of strategies and professional development activities to support your journey. You'll notice that some tools are more applicable to particular roles, such as that of the principal. Others will be useful to teacher-leaders, including instructional coaches, department chairs, or members of a site-based committee. There are a variety of tools, so you can choose the ones that work best in your situation.

The COMPASS Model

We find a compass to be a good metaphor for understanding the way that leaders can positively impact rigor in their school. A compass is an incredibly useful tool that can direct and guide you. Our COMPASS toolkit is the framework for the remaining chapters, one chapter for each point of the compass.

C – Creating a Positive and Supportive Culture

We've discovered that to make significant change in a school's program, a leader must understand the school's culture and incorporate strategies that will allow them to positively impact the culture.

When we talk about culture, we are talking about the complex set of values, traditions, and patterns of behavior present in a school. A school's culture reflects deeply held beliefs about students and schooling. Leaders recognize the importance of cultural symbols. They use these symbols to promote the institutional values and the school's core mission.

Successful leaders model the behaviors and practices that they expect others to use. It is important to use constructive language, support risk-taking, and build relationships. Chapter Three will discuss the importance of culture in more depth and provide strategies and tools that leaders can use to assure a culture supportive of the success of every student.

Tools in Chapter Three: Culture	
Tool 10	Rituals and Ceremonies: Name It, Claim It, and Explain It
Tool 11	Heroes and Heroines: Recognize the Right People
Tool 12	Stories and Tales: Turnaround Stories
Tool 13	Rewards and Reinforcements: Recognizing Rigor
Tool 14	Conduct a Self-Assessment
Tool 15	Conduct a Cultural Audit
Tool 16	Talk With and Learn From Your Teachers
Tool 17	Conduct a Cultural Assessment
Tool 18	Assessing Rigor in Your School's Culture
Tool 19	Make a Mental Adjustment: Change the Conversation

O – Ownership and Shared Vision

When all the critical stakeholders are engaged in the process, their collective commitment to the change is greater (David, 2009; Hord, 2009). When we work with teachers, families, and other school personnel, we almost always find that they have very different ideas about rigor and how it manifests itself in schools. These different ideas about rigor mean that it is important to involve each group in any discussion about increasing rigor in your school

Ownership and shared vision are one of the essential components of our COMPASS model and will be discussed in Chapter Four.

Tools in Chapter Four: Ownership and Shared Vision	
Tool 20	Assessing Facilitators and Barriers to Involvement
Tool 21	Determining Whom to Involve
Tool 22	Forming the Team and Getting Started
Tool 23	Building Consensus through "Fist to Five"
Tool 24	A Personal Vision of Rigor
Tool 25	Vision Letters
Tool 26	The Hot Air Balloon
Tool 27	Create or Recommit to a School-Wide Vision of Rigor
Tool 28	Another Approach to Visioning

M – Managing Data

Groups that use members' opinions as the primary source of data almost always become contentious. We've found that the most constructive groups are characterized by the gathering and analysis of data independent of any individual's experience or opinion.

It is essential to gather data about student learning to both analyze existing data and collect additional information to clarify or expand understanding. These and other strategies will be discussed in Chapter Five.

Tools in Chapter Five: Managing Data	
Tool 29	Narrow the Focus
Tool 30	Data Collection
Tool 31	Use an Outside Evaluator
Tool 32	Hold a Focus Group Meeting
Tool 33	Conduct a Student Shadow Study
Tool 34	Instructional Walkthrough
Tool 35	Look at Student Work
Tool 36	Data Source Analysis
Tool 37	Pattern Analysis
Tool 38	Force Field Analysis
Tool 39	Organize a Data Night
Tool 40	Planning Template for Setting Priorities and Goals

P – Professional Development

Also essential to improving rigor in your school's program is providing teachers and other staff with appropriate professional development. Leaders can set the direction for a school's professional development agenda. It is important that leaders model a commitment to continuous improvement and be active participants in professional development activities.

We've found that the most successful professional development is focused on increasing the capacity of the staff. The most successful models include a wider variety of activities, such as collaborative work teams, study groups, critical friends groups, peer coaching, and external support, such as partnerships and networks focused on specific knowledge and skills.

Chapter Six will explore the importance of professional development in more depth.

Tools in Chapter Six: Professional Development	
Tool 41	Assess Your Professional Development Efforts
Tool 42	Refining Your Professional Development
Tool 43	Professional Learning Communities: Assess Your Own Dispositions
Tool 44	Book Study
Tool 45	Looking at Student Work
Tool 46	Learning Walks
Tool 47	Lesson Studies
Tool 48	Charrette
Tool 49	Evaluating and Adjusting Curriculum
Tool 50	Aligning Expectations with High Standards
Tool 51	Develop Consistent Expectations
Tool 52	Choosing a Strategy
Tool 53	PRESS Forward Model for Action Planning

A – Advocacy

What leaders pay attention to becomes important (Schein, 2004) and it is important that school leaders are clear about their support for increased rigor. Advocacy is a way to press for changes in your school. It is also a way to build support for your vision of greater rigor and to secure resources to support your vision.

Successful advocacy is more than just having a passion for your vision to improve rigor. It requires developing a thoughtful and compelling message about the importance of rigor and identifying strategies to share your vision and mobilize support.

Chapter Seven will provide you with a set of useful tools that you can use to design your advocacy plan and to build support for your vision of a more rigorous school.

Tools in Chapter Seven: Advocacy	
Tool 54	Self-Assess Your Advocacy Skills
Tool 55	Seven Step Planning Process
Tool 56	Designing An Advocacy Plan
Tool 57	Stakeholders in Your School
Tool 58	Working with Internal Stakeholders
Tool 59	Movers and Shakers
Tool 60	Build a Network
Tool 61	The One Page Fact Sheet
Tool 62	Elevator Talk
Tool 63	Parent and Family Advocacy Tools
Tool 64	Advocacy with Your School Board
Tool 65	Dealing with the Media
Tool 66	Assessment of Technology
Tool 67	Advocacy Scorecard

S – Shared Accountability

We believe that one of the biggest roadblocks to improving rigor in schools is the resistance from teachers and parents. As we discussed earlier, every person deals with change differently. Some are more accepting, others more resistant.

No change is successful unless accountability is established. We suggest that teachers, families, and community, along with school leaders, are accountable for increasing rigor. Accountability is more than issuing mandates and forcing compliance. For school leaders, it involves energizing and motivating individuals as well as groups.

Shared accountability is critical to your efforts to improve rigor. Chapter Eight will discuss the issue in more depth and provide ideas that you can use in your school to build a collective commitment to the success of every student.

Tools in Chapter Eight: Shared Accountability	
Tool 68	Assess Your Work in This Area
Tool 69	Walkthroughs
Tool 70	Classroom Observations
Tool 71	Accountability through Professional Development
Tool 72	Analysis of School Improvement Plan
Tool 73	Accountability For Families and Community
Tool 74	Homework Help Tips for Parents
Tool 75	Ways to Support Student Accountability
Tool 76	Rigor through Requiring Demonstration of Learning

S – Structures

The day-to-day routines and structures of your school can impact your ability to become more rigorous. Structures, frequently rooted in past practice, can be major barriers to reform or they can be used to accelerate achieving your vision of a more rigorous school.

Structures that can support your efforts to become a more rigorous school will be examined in Chapter Nine. It is the final element of our COMPASS model.

Tools in Chapter Nine: Structures that Support Rigor	
Tool 77	Options for Collaborative Teams
Tool 78	Assess Your Professional Learning Community
Tool 79	Providing Collaborative Time
Tool 80	Plan for Use of Collaborative Time
Tool 81	Sample School Scheduling Strategies
Tool 82	Using Your School's Schedule to Increase Rigor
Tool 83	Schedules that Support Improved Rigor
Tool 84	Providing Value and Success for Students
Tool 85	Options for Motivating Students
Tool 86	Structures to Provide Extra Support
Tool 87	Structures to Support Families
Tool 88	Structures to Support the Leader

Moving Forward

People respond to change in many different ways. That is especially true when the conversation deals with rigor in schools. The leader's role is to help people navigate the journey, to provide the confidence that the future will be secure, and to assure that people will be supported throughout the change. The final chapter will discuss issues related to dealing with resistance, supporting faculty and staff, and moving into the future.

Tools in Chapter Ten: Moving Forward for Growth	
Tool 89	Supporting Teachers and Staff
Tool 90	Strategies for Dealing with Resistance
Tool 91	Concerns-Based Adoption Model
Tool 92	Assessing Needs
Tool 93	Have a Clear, Concrete Result
Tool 94	Celebrate Success
Tool 95	Assess Your Own Commitment
Tool 96	Change Attitudes
Tool 97	Self-Assessment of Focus on Students

Tool 1 – Check Your Own Assumptions

We all hold assumptions about things. Those assumptions are based on our experiences and reflect our own idiosyncratic experiences. In any group, its members bring to the conversation their own assumptions.

Tool 1   Check Your Own Assumptions

♦ What do you believe about rigor?

_____

_____

_____

_____

♦ What motivation strategies work most successfully with your school community?

_____

_____

_____

_____

♦ How quickly do you believe your school can become more rigorous?

_____

_____

_____

_____

♦ What conditions are most likely to result in a more rigorous school?

_____

_____

_____

_____

♦ Is your vision of rigor the one that should be implemented?

_____

_____

_____

_____

Final Thoughts

Most changes in schools take place in response to events (different students, societal trends). These events help to identify a need. Schools respond to these emerging needs in one of three ways: ignore them, reject them, or address them.

A starkly different approach is a much more thoughtful and deliberative planning process. We suggest that when you work with your community to increase rigor, it is best to use a deliberative process, one that involves important stakeholders, provides for discussion about approaches and strategies, utilizes a collaborative approach to making decisions, regularly collects data about progress, and develops capacity to sustain the work.

Tool 2 – Your Personal Vision

Before you move any further in *Rigor in Your School: A Toolkit for Leaders*, we'd like to ask you to stop and think about your vision for a rigorous school. If your school, classroom, or district were truly rigorous, what would that look like? How would your teachers and students be different? What would you be doing differently than you are today? Take a few moments, and sketch out your vision using Tool 2-Your Personal Vision. You can create your vision in narrative, bullet points, or diagrams. Keep it; you'll want to refer to it during Chapter Four: Ownership and Shared Vision.

Tool 2   Your Personal Vision

What does it look like? Sound like? What are teachers doing? What are students doing? What are you doing? What materials and resources have changed? How is this different from what is happening today?

_____

_____

_____

_____

_____

_____

_____

_____

_____

_____

_____

_____

_____

_____

_____

_____

_____

_____

2

Rigor, Research, and the Change Process

In this chapter, we'll address three key aspects of increasing rigor in your school. First, we'll look at the definition of rigor. There are as many viewpoints of rigor as there are sources, but we will explain the facets of our definition.

> Rigor is creating an environment in which each student is expected to learn at high levels, each student is supported so he or she can learn at high levels, and each student demonstrates learning at high levels.
>
> Barbara Blackburn, *Rigor is NOT a Four-Letter Word* (2008)

Next, we will provide professional development suggestions for researching the topic of rigor, as well as giving you a list of recommended resources for further study. Finally, we will turn our attention to the change process. For each of these, there are a variety of tools for your use.

Tools in Chapter Two: Rigor, Research, and the Change Model	
Tool 3	Rubric Reflections
Tool 4	Assessing Where You Are Now
Tool 5	Digging Deeper Into Research
Tool 6	Begin Your Planning
Tool 7	Implementation Planning Activities
Tool 8	Planning Activities for Sustaining Success
Tool 9	Evaluating and Adjusting Your Plan

Rigor

Probably the major concern we hear from leaders is "What exactly is rigor? How do I know if our classrooms are rigorous?" In *Rigor is NOT a Four-Letter Word*, Barbara defined rigor as "creating an environment in which each student is expected to learn at high levels, each student is supported so he or she can learn at high levels, and each student demonstrates learning at high levels" (Blackburn, 2008).

We want to focus on the total environment you create in your school. Our three-part view of rigor is not limited to the curriculum students are expected to learn. It is more than a specific lesson or instructional strategy. It is deeper than what a student says or does in response to a lesson. True rigor is the result of weaving together all elements of schooling to raise students to higher levels of learning.

This three-part approach assures that rigor doesn't consist of just adding curriculum requirements or raising grading standards. Integral to our model is providing every student with high levels of support so that they can thrive and be successful in their classrooms.

Expecting Students to Learn at High Levels

We've learned that rigor begins by *creating an environment in which each student is expected to learn at high levels.* Having high expectations starts with the decision that every student possesses the potential to be his or her best, no matter what.

Almost everyone we talk with says, "We have high expectations for our students." Sometimes that is evidenced by the behaviors in the school; at other times actions don't match the words. When you visit classrooms and work with your teachers, there are some ways you can assess the level of rigor.

As you work with teachers to design lessons that incorporate more rigorous opportunities for learning, you will want to consider the questions that are embedded in the instruction. Higher-level questioning is an integral part of a rigorous classroom. Look for open-ended questions, ones that are at the higher levels of Bloom's Taxonomy (analysis, synthesis).

It is also important to look at how teachers respond to student questions. When we visit schools it is not uncommon for teachers who ask higher-level questions to accept low level responses from students. In rigorous classrooms teachers push students to respond at high levels. They ask extending questions. If a student does not know the answer, the teacher continues to probe and guide the student to an appropriate answer, rather than moving on to the next student.

Supporting Students to Learn at High Levels

High expectations are important, but the most rigorous schools assure that *each student is supported so he or she can learn at high levels*, the second part of our definition. It is essential that teachers design lessons that move students to more challenging work while simultaneously providing ongoing scaffolding to support students learning as they reach those higher levels.

Providing additional scaffolding throughout lessons is one of the most important ways to support students. This can occur in a variety of ways, but it requires that teachers ask themselves during every step of their lesson, "What extra support might my students need?"

Provide Scaffolding in Lessons

> **Examples of Scaffolding Strategies**
> ♦ Guiding Questions
> ♦ Chunking Information
> ♦ Color-Coding Steps in a Project
> ♦ Writing Standards as Questions for Students to Answer
> ♦ Using Visuals and Graphic Organizers such as a Math Graphic Organizer for Word Problems
> ♦ Providing Tools such as Interactive Reading Guides, Guide-o-Ramas

Ensuring Students Demonstrate Learning at High Levels

The third component of a rigorous classroom provides *each student with opportunities to demonstrate learning at high levels.* We often hear that, "If teachers provide more challenging lessons that include extra support, then learning will happen." We've learned that if we want students to show us they understand what they learned at a high level, we also need to provide opportunities for students to demonstrate they have truly mastered that learning. One way to accomplish that is through increased student engagement.

Student engagement is a critical aspect of rigor. In too many classrooms, most of the instruction consists of the teacher-centered large group instruction, perhaps in an interactive lecture or discussion format. The general practice during these lessons is for the teacher to ask a question and then call on a student to respond. While this provides an opportunity for one student to demonstrate his or her understanding, the remaining students don't do so. Another option would be for the teacher to allow all students to respond either through pair-share, thumbs up or down, writing an answer on small whiteboards and sharing their response, or responding on a handheld computer that tallies responses. Such activities hold each student accountable for demonstrating their understanding.

Indicators of High-Levels of Student Engagement

Negative Indicators	Positive Indicators
◆ One student responds	◆ All students respond
◆ Two or three students discuss content	◆ All students discuss content in small groups
◆ Students are asked if they understand, with a simple yes or no and no probing	◆ All students write a response in a journal or exit slip

When you talk with your teachers about their instructional practices, you can also ask them about engagement and how they design lessons to promote positive student engagement and high-levels of student accountability for demonstrating their learning.

Tool 3 – Rubric Reflections

On the following pages, you'll find Tool 3A-Rubric for Gauging Progress Towards Rigor that describes the varying components of rigor. It was originally introduced in *Rigor is NOT a Four-Letter Word* to be used as a general tool and a starting point for discussions about rigor. Depending on your situation, you may want to start the process described below with your administrative team, school leadership or improvement teams, or all faculty and staff.

What if...

"Should I begin using the rubric with everyone, or should I start with my leadership team? Is there a best way?"

Good question. There is no one best strategy. You will want to consider your school, the faculty, and where you are on your journey to becoming more rigorous. We believe it is always important to build a cadre of leaders who can advocate for your vision. Therefore, you might want to start with your leadership team, or an informal group of teacher leaders. They will offer you advice about how you might use the rubric with the larger group.

Tool 3A Rubric for Gauging Progress Toward Rigor

	Starting at the Base	Making Progress Up the Mountain	Reaching New Heights
High Expectations for Learning	I am working to understand what it means to say that each student can learn, will learn, and I will help them do so.	I believe that each student can learn, will learn, and I will help them do so. I sometimes act on those beliefs or I act on those beliefs with some students.	I consistently act on my unwavering belief that each student can learn, will learn, and I will help them do so.
Support and Scaffolding	I sometimes provide support and scaffolding. This support is usually general and built into the regular lesson. At times, I provide optional extra help.	I sometimes provide the appropriate support and scaffolding students need to ensure their success. This support is customized for each student at times. At times, I provide optional extra help.	I regularly provide the support and scaffolding each student needs to ensure their success. This support is customized for each student and supports my belief that students are not allowed to not learn. It is appropriate and encourages independence. If extra help is needed, it is required, and is offered when the student can attend.
Demonstration of Learning	Occasionally, some students demonstrate understanding of content in a way that is appropriately challenging. More often than not, students prefer basic assignments or questions. Students are generally given one opportunity to show they have mastered content.	Sometimes, students are given the opportunity to show they understand content in a way that is appropriately challenging. Students are beginning to see the value of more challenging assessments. At times, I provide alternative assessments and will allow students to redo work.	Each student regularly demonstrates their understanding of content in ways that are appropriately challenging. In other words, students do not take the easy way out in terms of showing me they learned. I provide alternative ways for students to do this and allow those students who need it extra time or a second opportunity.
Level of Student Engagement	There are limited opportunities for students to be engaged in learning beyond listening and taking notes. Most of my instruction is directed toward the whole class. At times, I provide the opportunity for students to work with another student to apply their learning.	Some students are actively engaged in learning. There is a mix of whole group and small group/partner activities, and some activities are interactive. I facilitate some activities, and some ownership is shifted to students. However, the focus is still on me.	All students are actively engaged in learning. Each is participating in every aspect of the lesson by making connections, contributing to the discussion (whether small group, partner, or whole group), and responding to learning. The majority of the activities are interactive, and whole group activities are limited. I am the facilitator, and the focus for learning is on the students.

(continued)

Tool 3A   Rubric for Gauging Progress Toward Rigor *(continued)*

	Starting at the Base	Making Progress Up the Mountain	Reaching New Heights
Motivational Element: Value	I ask students to apply my lessons to their real lives. I make sure my students understand how my lesson applies to future tests they will take (such as standardized testing). I sometimes share with them why I think the content is important.	I sometimes design lessons that allow students to see the value. I incorporate real-life application activities into some of my lessons. If they volunteer, students can share their own applications of learning.	I design lessons that allow students to see the value of the specific learning. Application activities are woven seamlessly throughout the lesson. Students are given ample opportunity to make personal connections about relevance to their own lives and futures.
Motivational Element: Success	If the majority of my students aren't learning, I reteach the content of the lesson. Sometimes, I provide opportunities for students to come in for extra help if they want to. I expect my students to succeed, and I am learning how to help them understand that.	I build scaffolding into some lessons. I provide opportunities for students to come in for extra help when needed. I regularly tell my students that I expect them to succeed, and I try to help them make that a reality.	I build appropriate scaffolding and support into every lesson. Students know my focus is to remove barriers to their success. I require students to come in for extra help when needed, and I support them in positive ways that encourage growth and independent learning. All students know that we learn together, and that they can be successful.
Overall Classroom Culture	Members of our learning community (students, teachers, parents, etc.) are learning what it means to set a standard that not learning is unacceptable. We are also discussing how to move beyond grades to authentic learning. We celebrate some of our successes.	Some members of our learning community (students, teachers, parents, etc.) believe that it is unacceptable to not learn. We are learning to focus on learning in addition to grades. We celebrate success as well as progress.	Every member of our learning community (students, teachers, parents, etc.) believes that it is unacceptable to not learn. The focus is on learning at high levels, not just grades. We celebrate success as well as progress.

There are two options for using the rubric. You might begin by introducing the definition of rigor, as well as the full rubric. Next, discuss the criteria descriptions. Finally, using Tool 3B-Rubric Template for Gauging Progress Towards Rigor, ask all participants to rank each area and list examples to support their decision. You may want to give them an extended time, such as a week, to reflect and more fully complete this activity. Finally, discuss their perspectives to agree on where your school is on the road toward rigor.

The second option is to distribute the rubric without any discussion. Once participants have completed their rubrics and reflections, then discuss what they discovered. For more information on similar processes, see Chapter Four: Ownership and Shared Vision.

What if...

"How important are the examples on the rubric template?"

Examples are useful because they help us begin to assess your current progress. What is critically important is to make sure that there is clear evidence for the examples you cite. You will want to avoid talking in generalities and try to get really specific in what you see. For example, a teacher might believe that they hold high expectations for learning but cannot cite a specific verbal or nonverbal behavior that conveys that message to students. The more precise the example, the more useful it will be for your continued planning.

Tool 3B Rubric Template for Gauging Progress Toward Rigor

	Starting at the Base	Making Progress Up the Mountain	Reaching New Heights	Examples
High Expectations for Learning	I am working to understand what it means to say that each student can learn, will learn, and I will help them do so.	I believe that each student can learn, will learn, and I will help them do so. I sometimes act on those beliefs or I act on those beliefs with some students.	I consistently act on my unwavering belief that each student can learn, will learn, and I will help them do so.	
Support and Scaffolding	I sometimes provide support and scaffolding. This support is usually general and built into the regular lesson. At times, I provide optional extra help.	I sometimes provide the appropriate support and scaffolding students need to ensure their success. This support is customized for each student at times. At times, I provide optional extra help.	I regularly provide the support and scaffolding each student needs to ensure their success. This support is customized for each student and supports my belief that students are not allowed to not learn. It is appropriate and encourages independence. If extra help is needed, it is required, and is offered when the student can attend.	
Demonstration of Learning	Occasionally, some students demonstrate understanding of content in a way that is appropriately challenging. More often than not, students prefer basic assignments or questions. Students are generally given one opportunity to show they have mastered content.	Sometimes, students are given the opportunity to show they understand content in a way that is appropriately challenging. Students are beginning to see the value of more challenging assessments. At times, I provide alternative assessments and will allow students to redo work.	Each student regularly demonstrates their understanding of content in ways that are appropriately challenging. In other words, students do not take the easy way out in terms of showing me they learned. I provide alternative ways for students to do this and allow those students who need it extra time or a second opportunity.	

	Starting at the Base	Making Progress Up the Mountain	Reaching New Heights	Examples
Level of Student Engagement	There are limited opportunities for students to be engaged in learning beyond listening and taking notes. Most of my instruction is directed toward the whole class. At times, I provide the opportunity for students to work with another student to apply their learning.	Some students are actively engaged in learning. There is a mix of whole group and small group/partner activities, and some activities are interactive. I facilitate some activities, and some ownership is shifted to students. However, the focus is still on me.	All students are actively engaged in learning. Each is participating in every aspect of the lesson by making connections, contributing to the discussion (whether small group, partner, or whole group), and responding to learning. The majority of the activities are interactive, and whole group activities are limited. I am the facilitator, and the focus for learning is on the students.	
Motivational Element: Value	I ask students to apply my lessons to their real lives. I make sure my students understand how my lesson applies to future tests they will take (such as standardized testing). I sometimes share with them why I think the content is important.	I sometimes design lessons that allow students to see the value. I incorporate real-life application activities into some of my lessons. If they volunteer, students can share their own applications of learning.	I design lessons that allow students to see the value of the specific learning. Application activities are woven seamlessly throughout the lesson. Students are given ample opportunity to make personal connections about relevance to their own lives and futures.	

(continued)

Tool 3B Rubric Template for Gauging Progress Toward Rigor *(continued)*

	Starting at the Base	Making Progress Up the Mountain	Reaching New Heights	Examples
Motivational Element: Success	If the majority of my students aren't learning, I reteach the content of the lesson. Sometimes, I provide opportunities for students to come in for extra help if they want to. I expect my students to succeed, and I am learning how to help them understand that.	I build scaffolding into some lessons. I provide opportunities for students to come in for extra help when needed. I regularly tell my students that I expect them to succeed, and I try to help them make that a reality.	I build appropriate scaffolding and support into every lesson. Students know my focus is to remove barriers to their success. I require students to come in for extra help when needed, and I support them in positive ways that encourage growth and independent learning. All students know that we learn together, and that they can be successful.	
Overall Classroom Culture	Members of our learning community (students, teachers, parents, etc.) are learning what it means to set a standard that not learning is unacceptable. We are also discussing how to move beyond grades to authentic learning. We celebrate some of our successes.	Some members of our learning community (students, teachers, parents, etc.) believe that it is unacceptable to not learn. We are learning to focus on learning in addition to grades. We celebrate success as well as progress.	Every member of our learning community (students, teachers, parents, etc.) believes that it is unacceptable to not learn. The focus is on learning at high levels, not just grades. We celebrate success as well as progress.	

Tool 4 – Assessing Where You Are Now

Look at the definition of rigor: "Rigor is creating an environment in which each student is expected to learn at high levels, each student is supported so he or she can learn at high levels, and each student demonstrates learning at high levels (Blackburn, 2008)."

Point out four key words in the definition: environment, expected, supported, and demonstrates. These are the four critical elements of rigor: an environment that reflects and supports rigor, high expectations for each student, appropriate support to accompany the increased expectations, and a demonstration of learning from each student.

Ask participants (either individually or in small groups) to complete Tool 4A-Examples from Our School below, identifying examples of current practices that reflect each area. For example, what are specific examples of ways we have high expectations for students?

TOOL 4A Examples from Our School

	Examples that Currently Exist in Our School
Environment	
Expectations	
Support	
Demonstration of Learning	

Another way to approach this activity is to use posters with a large group. Create posters for the four keywords (environment, expectations, support, and demonstration of learning). As faculty enter a meeting, give each person four sticky notes. Describe the activity (see prior description) and ask them to post their examples anonymously, using one sticky note per poster. Next, ask them to discuss their responses in small groups, focusing on ideas they want to try in the future. Using a T-chart similar to Tool 4B-Comparing Examples, discuss current strengths in the school as well as possible future options.

Tool 4B   Comparing Examples

Environment	
How We Do This Now	**What We Want To Try**

High Expectations	
How We Do This Now	**What We Want To Try**

Support	
How We Do This Now	**What We Want To Try**

Demonstration of Learning	
How We Do This Now	**What We Want To Try**

What if...

"Our faculty spent a lot of time using the rubric and the definition to see where we are. But I'm still not sure if we really understand it. For example, we say we have high expectations, but how do we really know instead of just 'feeling like it'?"

The concept of rigor is complex, and so is each of the components. Prior to these self-assessment activities, you may want to review relevant research. This will give your stakeholders a deeper understanding of the definition, since it is founded on the available research.

Research

There is a wealth of research that is related to the concept of rigor. You can find a thorough review and summary in Chapter Two in *Rigor is NOT a Four-Letter Word* or *Rigorous Schools and Classrooms: Leading the Way*. However, you may find it helpful to ask teachers to move deeper. An excellent strategy is to form small study groups to investigate research.

Tool 5 – Digging Deeper Into Research

Depending on your situation, you may want to ask your leadership team or your entire faculty to participate in this activity. Divide participants into small groups. Ask each group to choose an area of research related to rigor (see chart for list of suggested resources) and "dig deeper." Next, have each group share what they learned with the larger group. Facilitate a discussion of the key points and/or common threads. Finally, ask the group to compare the research findings to their current experiences in order to consider next steps.

TOOL 5 Research Resources

ACT-www.act.org

Southern Regional Education Board-www.sreb.org

The College Board-www.collegeboard.org

National High School Alliance-www.hsalliance.org

Achieve-www.achieve.org

American Diploma Project-www.achieve.org/adp-network

Common Core Standards Initiative-www.corestandards.org

Rigorous Schools and Classrooms: Leading the Way (Chapter Two: A Rationale for Rigor)

Rigor is NOT a Four-Letter Word (Chapter One: The Case for Rigor)

The Change Process

Schools are constantly changing and improving—students change, families change, the community changes, expectations change, and the context in which the schools function changes.

Based on our work helping schools strengthen and improve, we developed our BASE model to describe this process. We chose BASE because everything you do to improve rigor must be built on a solid base, one that reflects research and best practice, builds support among teachers and families, and includes solid measures for success.

In Chapter One, we introduced our COMPASS model that includes seven key strategies you can use to improve rigor in your school. Much like the solid "base" for planning, we like the compass as a metaphor because a compass shows the way and always points to "true north." Compasses are most effective when they sit on a BASE, one that provides a firm and steady foundation.

The four stages of our BASE model reflect a commitment to continuous improvement.

BASE Model

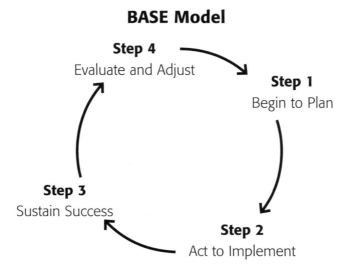

Our model is organized to provide four clear steps you can use to work with your teachers, families, and community to achieve your vision for a more rigorous school. You'll notice that it is circular and is built on an assumption that to nurture and sustain improvements in rigor, you must continue to examine how you've done. This analysis in turn will lead to identifying other ways you can make your school more rigorous.

Step 1: Begin to Plan

As you begin to think about planning, we want to emphasize the importance of using an inclusive process to make your vision of a more rigorous school a reality. We've discovered that involving others in planning is one of the most important tools. It allows people to develop collaborative skills, and to learn and grow together. Hearing different points-of-view can help assure that what is planned is most appropriate for your school.

There are also other critical aspects of the planning process that support your effort to improve the rigor of your school, such as agreeing on a vision or mission, assessing current available data, determining a process for decision-making, and deciding on methods for sharing information.

Because the COMPASS model sits on this strong base of planning and implementing change, the two are strongly connected. As such, many of the tools you will need for each stage are included in the COMPASS chapters. For each stage, we will ask you to think about the specific actions needed. Each action is posed in the form of a question. Think about your specific situation. If you can answer "Yes," then move on to the next action question. However, if your answer is "No" or "I'm not sure," consider using the recommended tools in the third column of the planning chart.

Tool 6 – Begin Your Planning

The first step is to begin planning. Use Tool 6-Begin Your Planning to guide your thinking.

Tool 6   Begin Your Planning

Planning Question	YES	NO or UNSURE
Are critical stakeholders involved?		See Tools 21 and 22 in Chapter Four
Is there an agreed upon mission/vision for a rigorous school?		See Tools 24–28 in Chapter Four
Do we have the data and information about our current conditions? Is there an agreed upon process for making decisions?		See Tools 36–39 in Chapter Five See Tool 23 in Chapter Four
How will we share information with others?		See Tools 60–64 in Chapter Seven

Step 2: Act to Implement the Plan

Planning is just the beginning. Implementing and sustaining changes can be even more of a challenge because it is the implementation that forces people to face the reality that things "may be different." Implementation often provokes a range of feelings including regret about abandoning familiar practices, exhilaration at the prospect of new ideas, or fear of being overwhelmed by the challenge of doing something new.

As you begin implementation, key strategies include creating a culture of collegiality, executing a clear strategy for collecting, assessing, and using data, preparing options for teachers to discuss successes and challenges regarding the implementation, having a clear decision-making process, and regularly sharing information in a systematic manner. Tool 7-Implementation Planning Activities will help you address these steps.

Tool 7   Implementation Planning Activities

Planning Question	YES	NO or UNSURE
Have you created a culture of collegiality?		See Tool 20 in Chapter Four, Tool 43 in Chapter Six, and Tools 79–82 in Chapter Nine
Do you have a process for gathering initial data about implementation and monitoring the implementation?		See Tools 30–39 in Chapter Five
What opportunities have you planned for teachers to talk about and share their successes and challenges?		See Tools 10 and 16 in Chapter Three
Is there an agreed upon process for making decisions?		See Tool 23 in Chapter Four
How will we share information with others?		See Tools 60–64 in Chapter Seven

What if...

"Despite all our planning, we've drifted off our focus. It seems that once the school year started, we had so many other things to do, this is taking a back seat. As a result, two of our faculty members have become very negative, saying, 'See, this is just one more thing to do. We don't really have time for it, and we didn't need to do it in the first place.'"

Your work to increase the rigor of your school should be based on a shared vision of quality teaching and learning. It is important to link every activity to the vision. The leader of a Chicago area school started every meeting with an opportunity for the group to review the vision and think about how what they were discussing contributed to achieving the vision. You can also talk about the vision with parents, with the community, and with staff. You might use your school website and newsletter to maintain focus on the vision.

Besides maintaining a focus on the vision, several leaders we know focus on gathering and sharing data about progress and success. They work with teachers to identify the measures that will be used to monitor progress and then are diligent about gathering and reporting the progress.

Step 3: Sustain Success

Change is more likely to be sustained when your work is guided by a shared vision, and where teachers and other school staff are actively involved in planning, implementing, and monitoring your progress. When change is the result of the personal vision of one or two people, the change is more likely to be abandoned as soon as its advocates leave.

The third part of our planning model focuses on sustaining success. At this stage you should continue to monitor the implementation and provide continued support for implementation. You should also work to build internal capacity with teacher leaders so that the commitment to increased rigor becomes an integral part of the way your school operates. Although several of the specific steps are similar to those in earlier stages, at this point, it is critical to ensure they are actually occurring, rather than simply being planned. Tool 8-Planning Activities for Sustaining Success is your guide.

Tool 8 Planning Activities for Sustaining Success

Planning Question	YES	NO or UNSURE
Do you have a strategy for monitoring the success of your plan, identifying next steps, and suggesting appropriate changes?		See Tools 21–22 and Tools 36–40 in Chapter Five
Is there time for teachers to work with colleagues to share successes and participate in professional development?		See Tools 10 and 16 in Chapter Three
What steps will you take to create a culture that will sustain the improvements?		See Tools 14, 15, and 17 in Chapter Three
How will you gather data and use that data to guide decisions?		See Tools 29–40 in Chapter Five
What is your plan for celebrating successes?		See Chapter Ten

Step 4: Evaluate and Adjust

The final stage of our BASE planning model is to "Evaluate and Adjust." We've come to appreciate that the best schools are those that are comfortable with routine evaluation of their program. They want to know what is going well and they are not afraid of identifying areas for further growth. This routine monitoring and adjusting is what sets them apart from other schools.

The planning process is circular and decisions you make during this step will naturally lead you to continue your planning to become even more rigorous. Tool 9-Evaluating and Adjusting Your Plan includes evaluating success and identifying next steps, ensuring that you sustain progress over time.

Tool 9   Evaluating and Adjusting Your Plan

Planning Question	YES	NO or UNSURE
Do you have a process to evaluate the success of your plan and identify next steps?		See Tools 36–40 in Chapter Five
Have you gathered the data to make informed decisions about your progress?		See Tools 30–25 in Chapter Five
What plans are developed for sharing your plans with teachers, families, and community?		See Tools 57–66 in Chapter Seven
What is your plan for celebrating successes?		See Chapter Ten

Final Thoughts and Action Planning

Schools continue to deal with pressure to immediately improve their students' education. This leads many schools to bounce from one improvement strategy to another without a clear vision and purpose, and without a clear sense of how they will measure progress and success.

Thoughtful planning is critical. It must occur collaboratively and in support of a shared vision about a more rigorous school. But planning alone is not sufficient. You must continue to monitor the implementation, examine data about your success, and make appropriate adjustments as needed. Take some time to draft out your action plan for this area.

My Action Plan for Understanding Rigor, Research, and the Change Process

The most important tool from this chapter in my current situation is:

_____

_____

_____

_____

_____

_____

_____

I also think the following concepts and/or tools would be useful in my situation:

_____

_____

_____

_____

_____

_____

_____

I need additional help or resources in the form of:

_____

_____

_____

_____

_____

_____

_____

My next action steps are to:

_____

_____

_____

_____

_____

_____

_____

3
Culture

The culture of a school is a powerful tool for shaping the behavior of those who work there because it reflects the important values and underlying assumptions of that school. Understanding culture is critical for educational leaders. Culture reflects the unspoken norms about schools, their purpose, and their organization and is reflected in the assumptions people hold about students, their learning, and the rigor of the instructional program. It is often described as "the way we do things around here" (Bower, 1996). Culture is a powerful set of rituals, traditions, and practices that are often transmitted without question from generation to generation.

Once you understand the varying aspects of your school culture, you can begin to shape the culture in ways that support your goals for a rigorous school. The tools in this chapter will help you assess your current culture and consider possible changes you would like to make.

Indicators of School Culture

Rituals and Ceremonies – These provide structure to our daily life and to the routine of a school. Rituals occur rather routinely while ceremonies are grander, less frequent events (i.e. graduation). Both rituals and ceremonies reflect values in their structure, their priority, and carry meaning about what is valued and what is important.

Heroes and Heroines – Those people who are looked up to as reflecting the organization's values; people who are examples of living the values.

Stories and Tales – Those recollections of events that are told and retold and play a powerful role in sharing examples of organizational values. Stories often contain morals and are inevitably engaging.

Rewards and Reinforcements – These reflect those things that are valued and therefore rewarded. Is it creativity in the classroom or compliance with established patterns? Is it waiving a rule so that a student may be successful or adhering to established policy?

Adapted from: Bolman & Deal (2003); Peterson & Deal (2002)

Developing the capacity to understand your school's culture, how it works, and how it can be shaped is an important strategy for school leaders. This chapter will introduce tools that you can use to work with your school community to build and nurture a culture that supports a rigorous academic experience for every student.

Tools in Chapter Three: Culture	
Tool 10	Rituals and Ceremonies: Name It, Claim It, and Explain It
Tool 11	Heroes and Heroines: Recognize the Right People
Tool 12	Stories and Tales: Turnaround Stories
Tool 13	Rewards and Reinforcements: Recognizing Rigor
Tool 14	Conduct a Self-Assessment
Tool 15	Conduct a Cultural Audit
Tool 16	Talk With and Learn From Your Teachers
Tool 17	Conduct a Cultural Assessment
Tool 18	Assessing Rigor in Your School's Culture
Tool 19	Make a Mental Adjustment: Change the Conversation

Tool 10 – Rituals and Ceremonies: Name It, Claim It, and Explain It

One way to celebrate a culture of rigor is to use "Name It, Claim It, and Explain It." As you see an example of rigorous instruction in a classroom, take a digital picture or video of what occurs. Then, begin each of your faculty meetings by projecting the picture or video. Explain to your faculty, "I saw something great related to rigor this week. It's up here on the screen. If it belongs to you, stand up and name what you did, claim it as yours, and explain what you were doing." With this tool, you celebrate something positive related consistently in your meetings.

Tool 11 – Heroes and Heroines: Recognize the Right People

Every school has heroes and heroines among its students and staff. They are people who are admired by others in the school for how they go about their work and live their lives.

But there are both positive and negative examples. There are people who are admired for their commitment to the school's values and beliefs or to a vision of a more rigorous school. Then there are those who are admired because they are cynical or pessimistic.

As a leader, you want to reinforce the people who reflect your school's commitment to increased rigor. You can do that by recognizing people who reflect the vision and experienced success.

A high school principal in Tacoma, WA took photos of classroom and student activities throughout the year. The photos captured students and teachers doing things that supported the school's vision. The photos were hung in the hallway and other public places and served as a visual recognition of the schools heroes and heroines.

When Mill Creek Middle School was constructed, an old rowboat and an oar were found on the site. The principal hung the boat in the main office and used the oar to recognize teachers for their exceptional commitment to the success of students. Every month, the oar is awarded to one teacher who "goes over and above" to support students. Dressed as an old boatman, the principal enters the teacher's class and recognizes his or her accomplishments. The oar remains in the class for that month as a visual reminder of the teacher's commitment to the students.

Tool 11   Heroes and Heroines: Recognize the Right People

Consider your school, its students, and employees.

♦ How do you celebrate people who reflect your school's commitment to increased rigor?

_____

_____

_____

_____

_____

_____

_____

_____

♦ What strategies might you use to recognize the heroes and heroines of your school?

_____

_____

_____

_____

_____

_____

_____

_____

Tool 12 – Stories and Tales: Turnaround Stories

In every school, teachers, parents, students, and administrators tell stories about memorable people or events. Stories are powerful because they convey the history of the school and reflect the school's priorities and values.

We met a principal in suburban Phoenix who used stories to mold the culture of his school. When he arrived, teachers and families talked about the challenges faced by students and how this negatively impacted learning. As he listened to the stories, he recognized that the stories shaped expectations for students.

He set out to change the culture of his school by identifying "turnaround" stories, true stories of students who had persevered and made significant improvement in their learning. He also gathered stories about families and teachers who contributed to this success.

Whenever possible, he told one of his stories at both formal and informal meetings with parents, with members of the community, and with other administrators in the district. He began each faculty meeting with a "turnaround" story.

TOOL 12   Stories and Tales: Turnaround Stories

Think about your school and the stories that are told about your students, your families, and your teachers.

♦ What messages do these stories convey about your school and its students?

_____

_____

_____

_____

_____

_____

♦ What message do you want to convey?

_____

_____

_____

_____

_____

_____

♦ What stories can you tell about students, families, and teachers that would help shape an image of your school as rigorous and challenging for students?

_____

_____

_____

_____

_____

_____

Tool 13 – Rewards and Reinforcements: Recognizing Rigor

It's important to reward teachers who are leading or supporting increased levels of rigor. A simple way to do this is to keep a pad of "Recognizing Rigor" certificates (Tool 13-Rewards and Reinforcements: Recognizing Rigor) with you, so you can use them to acknowledge a teacher's work when conducting learning walks.

We'd also recommend you encourage teachers to use the certificates. Give each teacher a handful and keep some near teacher mailboxes. As you model the use of the awards, promote the idea that everyone can and should recognize efforts toward increasing rigor.

TOOL 13   Rewards and Reinforcements: Recognizing Rigor

Recognizing Rigor

_____   (your name)
recognized rigor today in

_____'s classroom.

(insert your description here) _____

_____

was an excellent example of:

_____   expecting each student to learn at high levels.

_____   supporting each student to learn at high levels.

_____   each student demonstrating learning at high levels.

_____   creating as environment that supports rigor.

Thank you!

Tool 14 – Conduct a Self-Assessment

You may want to assess the indicators of culture in your school. Think about your school, its routines, and organization. We've provided a set of questions using the four indicators of school culture. How might you use these elements to improve the educational rigor at your school? Tool 14A-Leadership Self-Assessment provides a version for you and your leadership team; Tool 14B-Stakeholder Self-Assessment gives you an option for faculty, staff, and other stakeholders.

What if...

"While completing the self-assessment, I realized that our actions don't reflect what we say we believe. For example, I emphasize that rigor is about supporting every student, but I also gave a leadership role to a teacher who believes that rigor is about assigning the most homework or having the highest number of failing grades among students. How do I begin to lead change so that our culture matches our vision for the future?"

What leaders do and how they act sends a powerful message about what is important. Who you select as a leader lets everyone know what you value and whether you are willing to challenge some long-standing practices. As principal, you have an opportunity to be very clear about your vision when you appoint people to roles, when you organize professional development, when you allocate budget, and when you create the schedule and assign classes. Think of each of these as a tool, a lever you can employ to let people know what is important.

Tool 14A Leadership Self-Assessment

	Guiding Questions	Examples from Your School
Rituals and Ceremonies	♦ What are the routines and rituals in your school? What values do they represent? ♦ Are there special ceremonies or events at your school? What do they celebrate? ♦ What messages do you communicate in your daily actions, classroom visits, and other interactions with members of your school community?	
Heroes and Heroines	♦ Who are the heroes or heroines on your staff? Why are they recognized? ♦ What ways do you identify and celebrate people who contribute to the success of every student? Who has high expectations for student success?	
Stories and Tales	♦ How do you communicate verbally and through your actions with your faculty and staff? What underlying messages are represented? ♦ What are the stories you tell about your school, its students, and staff? What stories do you encourage others to tell?	
Rewards and Reinforcements	♦ How do you recognize and reward teachers? What values are recognized and rewarded? Are these strategies successful? ♦ Do you routinely reward teachers, staff, and students who make exceptional efforts to improve student learning?	

TOOL 14B   Stakeholder Self-Assessment

	Guiding Questions	**Examples from Your School**
Rituals and Ceremonies	◆ What are the routines and rituals in your school? What values do they represent? ◆ Are there special ceremonies or events at your school? What do they celebrate? ◆ What messages does the leadership in the school communicate in their daily actions, classroom visits, and other interactions with you and other members of your school community?	
Heroes and Heroines	◆ Who are the heroes or heroines on your staff? Why are they recognized? ◆ What ways do the leaders in the school identify and celebrate people who contribute to the success of every student? Who has high expectations for student success?	
Stories and Tales	◆ How does your school leader communicate verbally and through his or her actions with you and/or other faculty and staff? What underlying messages are represented? ◆ What are the stories your school leaders tell about your school, its students, and staff? What are the stories you tell about your school, its students, and staff? ◆ What stories does your school leader encourage others to tell? What stories do you encourage others to tell?	
Rewards and Reinforcements	◆ How does your school recognize and reward teachers? What values are recognized and rewarded? Are these strategies successful? ◆ Do your school leaders routinely reward teachers, staff and students who make exceptional efforts to improve student learning?	

Collect and collate the responses from faculty and other stakeholders in your building. As we've said before, it is critical that you honor the anonymity of results, so only use this information to look at the overall perception of the culture of your school. Compare the perceptions of your stakeholders with your own assessment. How are they similar? How do they differ? Use this information and Tool 14C-Planning Next Steps to determine appropriate changes to make.

Tool 14C Planning Next Steps

	Guiding Questions	**Examples from Your School**
Rituals and Ceremonies	◆ What are the routines and rituals that you want to incorporate into your school? ◆ Are there special ceremonies or events you want to replace, change, or add? ◆ Do you want to adjust your communication in your daily actions, classroom visits, and other interactions with members of your school community? How?	
Heroes and Heroines	◆ Who should be heroes or heroines on your staff? How will you recognize them? ◆ How will you identify and celebrate people who contribute to the success of every student? Who has high expectations for student success?	
Stories and Tales	◆ How do you communicate verbally and through your actions with your faculty and staff? What underlying messages are represented? ◆ What are the stories you tell about your school, its students, and staff? What stories do you encourage others to tell?	
Rewards and Reinforcements	◆ How do you recognize and reward teachers? What values are recognized and rewarded? Are these strategies successful? ◆ Do you routinely reward teachers, staff, and students who make exceptional efforts to improve student learning?	

Many leaders recognize the power of a school's culture to shape the patterns of behavior and the interaction between teachers and students, and between teachers and administrators.

One way that leaders can quickly assess the culture of their school is to walk through the school, talk with students and teachers, and look at their own priorities. Tool 15A-Cultural Audit for Leaders provides a format for gathering that information and using it to guide your planning.

This tool can provide you with information that can guide the discussion of culture with your teachers and other school staff. It provides a quick and easy way to assess the current state of your school's culture and to determine appropriate next steps.

You can also ask teachers and other members of your school community to complete an assessment of the culture, using Tool 15B-Cultural Audit for Teachers and Stakeholders.

There are many different ways to gather data about your school's culture. Rather than using Tool 15, you might want to use Tool 16 to talk with your school leadership team about culture. Tool 17 provides another tool that can be used to gather both quantitative and qualitative data from people about your school's culture.

Tool 15 – Conduct a Cultural Audit

Another way to conduct a quick assessment of your school's culture is to observe patterns, talk with both students and staff, and consider your own behavior. Tool 15A-Cultural Audit for Leaders provides a format for this assessment.

You can also ask teachers and other members of your school community to complete an assessment, using Tool 15B-Cultural Audit for Teachers and Stakeholders.

What if....

"My perception of the school doesn't match what others say. I'm not talking about one or two stakeholders; most responses are different from mine. What do I do next?"

First, don't argue or become confrontational. Use the differences as an opportunity to open the conversation about the school and its priorities. You might want to gather information from students and families or you may want to use other data like grades and achievement scores to add to the conversation. For example, "If we believe in the value of rigorous work, what evidence do we see that says that is true?" Or you might ask, "If families don't believe our school is sufficiently rigorous, what might we do to modify that perception?"

Tool 15A   Cultural Audit for Leaders

Observe Patterns		
Guiding Questions	**Observations**	**Changes to Consider**
Walk the halls of your school. What do you see? What artifacts are visible that convey messages about student success? About the value of rigorous work? About a commitment to not accepting failure?		

Talk with Students and Staff		
Guiding Questions	**Observations**	**Changes to Consider**
Talk with a cross-section of teachers or students. What gets them excited about their work? About their learning? What do they find joy in?		

Consider Your Behavior		
Guiding Questions	**Observations**	**Changes to Consider**
Consider the last three months. What have you done to show your enthusiasm for learning? For student success? How have you recognized and rewarded students and staff?		

Tool 15B   Cultural Audit for Teachers and Stakeholders

Observe Patterns		
Guiding Questions	**Observations**	**Changes to Consider**
Walk the halls of your school. What do you see? What artifacts are visible that convey messages about student success? About the value of rigorous work? About a commitment to not accepting failure?		

Talk with Students and Staff		
Guiding Questions	**Observations**	**Changes to Consider**
Talk with a cross-section of other teachers or students. What gets them excited about their work? About their learning? What do they find joy in?		

Consider Your Behavior		
Guiding Questions	**Observations**	**Changes to Consider**
Consider the last three months. How has the leadership of your school shown enthusiasm for learning? For student success? How have they recognized and rewarded students and staff?		

Tool 16 – Talk With and Learn From Your Teachers

Earlier we said that a school's culture reflects the complex set of values, traditions, assumptions, and patterns of behavior that guide the behavior of those who work there. These patterns of behavior are often "unwritten" and comprise the agreed upon norms passed down from generation to generation. Often people are unaware of the underlying values until they are asked to stop, think about, and reflect on what beliefs shape and guide their behavior.

It can be helpful to provide an opportunity for teachers to talk about culture. At a staff meeting, ask each person to list five adjectives that describe your school's culture. Then, in small groups, ask them to organize the words into common themes. Share with the entire group and discuss their meaning. Ask groups to generate examples for the themes.

What if...

"We tried to talk about our school culture in a faculty meeting, but not everyone agreed on the descriptors. Several teachers dominated the discussion, and others wouldn't say anything. I thought we would be able to talk about the items and seek agreement, but we never got that far."

Don't give up. Most groups hold a variety of points-of-view and often disagree about the meaning of the descriptors of culture. You might want to have the discussion in a smaller group, like your leadership team. You can then use their ideas to guide a discussion with the entire faculty. Or you might consider structuring the discussion so that people work in small groups to promote greater participation. You could then use a modified jigsaw activity to allow people to process and react to the ideas.

Tool 17 – Conduct a Cultural Assessment

We often find it helpful to conduct a quick assessment of the culture in schools where we work. Tool 17-Conduct a Cultural Assessment provides a quick overview of your school culture. You can use the survey for self-assessment or with teachers, staff, or other stakeholders.

Tool 17   Conduct a Cultural Assessment

Directions: Rate each item using this scale:
1 = Never, 2 = Rarely, 3 = Sometimes, 4 = Often, 5 =Almost Always

Collegiality	Rating	Evidence
Our school reflects a true "sense of community."		
Teachers and staff tell stories and celebrate our school's values.		
Our schedule provides opportunities for teachers and staff to work together and communicate with one another.		
We have a tradition of rituals and celebrations that recognize our accomplishments.		
Teachers and staff appreciate the sharing of new ideas.		
Efficacy	**Rating**	**Evidence**
Members of our school community are interdependent and value one another.		
When something is not working in our school, the teachers and staff make changes rather than react passively.		
Our school community seeks alternatives to problems rather than continuing to do things we've always done.		
Rather than blame others, we work to define and solve problems.		
People work here because they enjoy and choose to be here.		
Professional Collaboration	**Rating**	**Evidence**
Teachers and staff talk about instructional strategies and curricular issues.		
Planning time is used to work together rather than work as individuals.		
The Student Code of Conduct is the result of collaboration among the staff.		
Teachers and staff work together to develop the school schedule.		
Teachers and staff are empowered to make instructional decisions rather than waiting for direction.		

Scoring: Tally the ratings you gave the fifteen items. Total scores will range from 15 to 75. The following suggests the status of your school culture.

      15–30   *There's Work to Be Done*: Conduct a more comprehensive assessment of your school's culture and invest resources in repairing and healing the culture.

      31–45   *Modifications Needed*: Begin with a more intense look at your culture to determine areas most in need of improvement.

      46–60   *You're on the Right Path*: You're in good shape, but need to continue to monitor your culture and make needed adjustments.

      61–75   *You're in Good Shape!* You have a positive culture, but need to monitor your school to maintain your momentum.

Adapted from: School Culture Triage, Center for Improving School Culture (CISC) http://www.schoolculture.net/triage.html

Tool 18 – Assessing Rigor in Your School's Culture

In Chapter Two, we shared our three-part definition of rigor: high expectations, high support, and student demonstration of learning at high levels. In Tool 18-Assessing Rigor in Your School's Culture, we supply focus questions and characteristics to allow you an in-depth consideration of rigor in your school. This can be used with leaders, teachers, and other stakeholders. For more information on the focus questions, see Chapter Three: Recognizing Rigor in *Rigorous Schools and Classrooms: Leading the Way* (2010).

TOOL 18 Assessing Rigor in Your School's Culture

Expectations of Student Learning		
	Focus Question	**Examples**
Challenging Curriculum	Is our curriculum challenging for all learners?	
High Level Instruction	Do we consistently provide high levels of instruction for all students?	
Adult Behaviors	Do our behaviors, as adults, encourage students to rise to new levels of learning?	
Support for Student Learning		
	Focus Question	**Examples**
Scaffolding	Do we consistently provide appropriate scaffolding within lessons on an ongoing basis?	
Incorporating Motivation	Do we consistently incorporate motivational elements into lessons?	
Addressing Strategic Knowledge	Do we intentionally teach and reinforce strategic knowledge, in addition to content knowledge?	
Providing Extra Help	Do we provide mandatory opportunities for extra help for those who need additional support, as well as optional times for any student who desired it?	

(continued)

Demonstration of Student Learning		
	Focus Question	**Examples**
Increased Student Engagement	Do we consistently engage students at high levels throughout lessons?	
Clear Standards and Rubrics	Do we provide clear standards and rubrics so students understand the expectations we have?	
Challenging Assessments	Are our assessments challenging to students? Do we define challenging by criteria other than grades or the number of students who fail a test?	
Multiple Options to Demonstrate Learning	Do we provide multiple options for students to demonstrate their understanding of content? Do we move beyond standardized testing for this?	

What if...

"I thought we were on the same page about rigor, but when we started discussing the various aspects of rigor, I realized that several of our teachers still believe rigor is about doing more work. What should I do now?"

Continue the conversation. It is not unusual to have this diversity. You may want to work with those who are most enthusiastic about your vision while at the same time continuing to engage the resistors in conversation about their work. In many cases, teachers don't have models of rigor that isn't focused on "doing more work." Some of your more enthusiastic teachers may be willing to share. Or you could start every meeting by sharing an example you observed when visiting classrooms.

Tool 19 – Make a Mental Adjustment: Change the Conversation

The stories people tell and their recollection of events play a powerful role in shaping your school's culture. Successful school leaders recognize the power of words to shape culture. Our thoughts drive our feelings and our actions. In *The Principalship from A to Z* (2009) we suggested a focus on the positive, the progress you make every day. We called that a "mental adjustment" and we encourage you to work with your teachers to "make a mental adjustment" in how you think about your school.

First, introduce the idea of a "mental adjustment" to your faculty. Use Tool 19-Examples of Mental Adjustments to give examples of negative thoughts. Brainstorm ways to turn those into positive thoughts. Tool 19-Examples of Mental Adjustments gives you examples of the transformed thoughts. Ask them to collect examples of negative thoughts and comments over a specified time period, such as one week.

Tool 19 Examples of Mental Adjustments

From Negative Thoughts	To Positive Thoughts
Why aren't our parents more involved?	What can we do to make our parents feel welcome?
Why doesn't our community value what we do?	How can we show the community we value them?
Why won't my students do their homework?	How can I include interesting and engaging activities in my lessons?
How can I get my students to learn this content?	How can we present the material so that it facilitates deep learning?
Why don't our students care about school?	What can we do to help our students become more interested in school?
Why isn't it possible to keep people happy?	What can I do today to have a positive interaction with everyone I meet?
How am I going to get everything done?	What am I going to do today that will make progress on my "to do" list?
Why can't all of our students meet standards?	How will I make a positive impact on one student today?

Next, work with faculty in small groups to prepare a list of prevalent "negative" thoughts. At a faculty meeting, share the list of "negatives" and ask people to work in small groups to convert them into "positive" statements. Share the "positives" and talk about how you can support one another in changing the conversation in your school.

Final Thoughts and Action Planning

Every school has a culture and it is a powerful tool for shaping the behavior of those who work at and attend the school. Because culture is such an amorphous concept, people often don't question the underlying beliefs and values that guide the culture. These tools are designed to provoke discussion about your school's culture and to use that conversation to help improve your school's commitment to a rigorous educational experience for every student.

My Action Plan for Impacting the Culture in My School

The most important tool from this chapter in my current situation is:

_____

_____

_____

_____

_____

I also think the following concepts and/or tools would be useful in my situation:

_____

_____

_____

_____

_____

I need additional help or resources in the form of:

_____

_____

_____

_____

_____

My next action steps are to:

_____

_____

_____

_____

_____

4

Ownership and Shared Vision

Efforts to increase the rigor of schools and classrooms are only successful when they have widespread support and ownership. They aren't as successful when the school or central office mandates rigor. We've learned that involving all stakeholders, families, and community, as well as teachers and other staff, is essential to your success. Participation and involvement help to build collective commitment to improving your school.

What if...

"Increasing rigor in our school is a mandated goal. How can I balance that mandate with stakeholder involvement?"

Rather than see the mandate as a barrier, use it as an opportunity to engage your teachers and other stakeholders in work that focuses on changes at your school. You might ask your school improvement team to help select a professional development model or you might ask your curriculum leaders or department chairs to work with you to identify the first steps you will take to become a more rigorous school. Tools 91 and 92 in Chapter Ten deal with overcoming resistance. You may also want to review the information about Maslow's hierarchy of needs in Tools 93 and 94, also in Chapter Ten, for some ideas about the needs individuals will have with a mandated change.

There is no perfect way to involve stakeholders in the discussion about rigor; however, we've learned that their participation must be authentic. The tasks must be real and their involvement valued. When you involve others in decision-making, it is important to understand some of the things that support involvement as well as the things that may inhibit your efforts.

Tools in Chapter Four: Ownership and Shared Vision	
Tool 20	Assessing Facilitators and Barriers to Involvement
Tool 21	Determining Whom to Involve
Tool 22	Forming the Team and Getting Started
Tool 23	Building Consensus through "Fist to Five"
Tool 24	A Personal Vision of Rigor
Tool 25	Vision Letters
Tool 26	The Hot Air Balloon
Tool 27	Create or Recommit to a School-Wide Vision of Rigor
Tool 28	Another Approach to Visioning

Tool 20 – Assessing Facilitators and Barriers to Involvement

Before determining who to involve in aspects of decision-making, it's important to consider the facilitators and barriers to involvement. At a basic level, a facilitator for each possible participant is the willingness to participate. Conversely, a lack of desire to be involved is a barrier. For some of your stakeholders, the barrier may be circumstance-dependent. For example, a faculty member with a new baby may not have the time or energy to take a leadership role right now. However, the same teacher may be more than willing to train new faculty the following year. We also worked with one school where one teacher wanted to chair the rigor committee. He was the ideal choice, but because he was also developing a new curriculum and pacing guide for the district, he asked to serve on the committee without chairing it.

From a broader perspective, there are a variety of facilitators and barriers to involvement for you to consider prior to asking individuals to participate.

Tool 20A Facilitators and Barriers

Facilitators	Barriers
♦ Adequate time to meet, talk about rigor, plan, implement, and assess current efforts. Lots of time may be required initially to get started.	♦ Little or no professional development provided about collaborative work.
♦ Clear understanding of the areas/topics that the group can address.	♦ Limits of decision-making authority are unclear or undefined.
♦ Appropriate, ongoing professional development for all stakeholders, including conflict management and decision-making skills.	♦ Principal directs and tells rather than guides.
♦ Accountability and responsibility of participants.	♦ Only the principal or superintendent held accountable for decisions.
♦ Availability of technical assistance.	♦ Group does not have power to make "real" decisions and gets mired in unimportant details.
♦ Comfort and support of the principal.	

Tool 20B-Assess Your Facilitators and Barriers allows you to assess the specific facilitators and barriers in your school. You can also use with stakeholders to obtain their perspective.

Tool 20B Assess Your Facilitators and Barriers

Area	Is this a facilitator or a positive characteristic in your school?	Is this a barrier or a negative characteristic in your school?	Examples, evidence, or thoughts.
Time to meet, talk, plan, implement, and assess.			
Clear understanding of the topic/area to address.			
Professional development.			
Accountability, responsibility, and/ or decision-making power of stakeholders.			
Availability of support or assistance when needed.			
Relationship of principal or other leaders with faculty.			

Ownership Tools

When you begin to work with your stakeholders on your shared vision of a more rigorous school you will want to consider whom to involve, the structure of the group, and the method of making decisions.

Tool 21 – Determining Whom to Involve

Deciding whom to involve in a project is critical. If people have a stake in the outcome of the decision, they should be represented. Be sure to involve those who have needed expertise. If a person or group is indifferent or has no expertise, their involvement might be very limited. It is important to engage everyone in the conversation. Seek to include every voice, particularly the missing voices of those who are often reluctant to speak out on issues. We've provided simple questions to help you assess appropriate levels of involvement for your personnel.

Tool 21A   Questions to Consider

Involve	Does this person have a stake in the outcome and have some level of expertise?
Don't Involve	Is this person indifferent to the outcome and does he/she have no expertise?
Limited Involvement	Does the person have concerns about the outcome, but lack expertise, or is he/she indifferent to the outcome?

Adapted From: Hoy and Tarter (2008)

Using Tool 21B-Thinking About Whom to Involve, draft your ideas about the involvement level of each of your stakeholders.

Tool 21B   Thinking About Whom to Involve

Group or Focus Area		
Involve	**Don't Involve**	**Limited Involvement**

Tool 22 – Forming the Team and Getting Started

Before you begin your work, you will also want to be clear about the purpose of the group, about membership, about communication, and about how decisions will be made. Tool 22A-Checklist for Formation of Collaboration Teams is a helpful reminder of the tasks to be tended to as the group begins its work.

Tool 22A   Checklist for Formation of Collaboration Teams

_____   Is the purpose clear? Is the role well defined?

_____   Is membership representative? Is membership appropriate to the task?

_____   Are there agreed upon norms for operation? For decision-making?

_____   Is there a mechanism to communicate with the larger school community? With other decision-making groups?

_____   What is the process for concluding the team's work?

From: Williamson and Blackburn (2010), *Rigorous Schools and Classrooms: Leading the Way*

What if...

"I have what many would consider to be a good problem. I have so many energetic, talented people...it's almost too many! How do I choose between too many good people?"

Lucky you! Most principals would love to have your problem. When we've worked with principals and teachers we've found that a sure way to dampen enthusiasm is to limit the opportunities for involvement. A principal in Michigan organized his "enthusiastic" teachers into smaller work groups, each working on a different area of interest. She found this kept people engaged and invested in improvement. An Illinois principal created a "Steering Committee" to monitor the work deal with recommendations from five work groups that dealt with specific areas of interest. This allowed most of the staff to be involved and created a mechanism to synthesize recommendations that might overlap or conflict with one another.

Tool 22B-Thinking About Forming Your Team allows you to move beyond the checklist to a more in-depth process for team formation.

Tool 22B   Thinking About Forming Your Team

Guiding Questions	Your Response
What is the purpose of the group or the purpose of the task?	
What is the role of each member of the group?	
Is membership representative? If any group is not represented, what adjustments need to be made?	
What are the strengths of the members of the group related to the task?	
What are the agreed upon norms for operation? For decision-making?	
How will this group communicate with the larger school community? With other decision-making groups?	
What is the process for concluding the team's work?	

Tool 23 – Building Consensus through "Fist to Five"

The goal of your work with stakeholders is to develop agreement about your vision for a more rigorous school. Consensus is often the preferred way to make decisions, but consensus can often be fleeting. It doesn't mean that everyone agrees wholeheartedly with the decision, but it does mean that everyone can support the decision. At a minimum, everyone should agree they can live with the decision.

When you use Tool 23-Building Consensus through "Fist to Five," ask every participant to indicate the level of support, from a closed fist (no support) to all five fingers (enthusiastic support). Ideally, continue the process until everyone holds up at least three fingers. This tool helps a group to seek common ground and is an easy way to assess the opinion of every participant.

TOOL 23   Building Consensus through "Fist to Five"

Fist	"I need to talk more on the proposal and require changes to support it."
1 Finger	"I still need to discuss some issues and I will suggest changes that should be made."
2 Fingers	"I am moderately comfortable with the idea but would like to discuss some minor things."
3 Fingers	"I'm not in total agreement but feel comfortable to let this idea pass without further discussion."
4 Fingers	"I think it's a good idea and will work for it."
5 Fingers	"It's a great idea and I will be one of those working to implement it."

Adapted From: Adventure Associates, 2009

What if...

"I like this idea, but I'm concerned. What if everyone shows a closed fist? What do I do then?"

We've worked with lots of groups all across the country and never encountered this, but it is not uncommon to have a lot of initial concern about a topic. When there are a lot of closed fists it means you need to continue the discussion. You might ask those with fists to describe their concerns or to share the questions they continue to have about the idea. You might also want to talk with your leadership team or informal teacher leaders to gather additional information about the concern. Sometimes the concern can be addressed by being clearer about what the idea means and the impact on teachers.

Visioning Tools

One of the most important things you can do as a leader is have a clear vision for your school. All schools have a vision, often written, but occasionally unwritten and unspoken. Beyond a general vision of the school, it is important to develop a shared vision to creating a more rigorous school.

Tool 24 – A Personal Vision of Rigor

Your personal vision consists of the most fundamental beliefs you hold about life, about your work, and about relationships with people. Because of this, it is not easy to write a personal vision statement. Before you can work with others to develop a shared vision, it is important to have your own personal vision. As a starting point, go back to the vision you drafted at the end of Chapter One. Now, using Tool 24A-Developing a Personal Vision, add details. Then, using Tool 24B-My Personal Vision Statement, complete your draft.

Tool 24A Developing a Personal Vision

Step 1: Think about your school. Make a list of what you would like to achieve as you make it more rigorous. Describe what it looks like and feels like.	
Step 2: Consider the following things about what you have written: relationships, personal interests, and community. Examine each item in your list to ensure that it still fits.	
Step 3: Develop a list of priorities. Identify the most important. Once this is done, review the list and rank them from most to least important. Remove the least important. Re-rank if appropriate. Check for relevance with your earlier list. Eliminate any item that is not relevant.	

(continued)

Tool 24A   Developing a Personal Vision

Step 4: Use the items from the first three steps to develop a personal vision statement. Review and edit the statement as often as needed until you believe it accurately reflects your commitment to more rigorous schools and classrooms.	

Adapted from: Williamson & Blackburn (2009). *The Principalship from A to* Z. Larchmont, NY: Eye on Education.

Tool 24B   My Personal Vision Statement

Step 1: Think about your school. Make a list of what you would like to achieve as you make it more rigorous. Describe what it looks like and feels like.

_____

_____

_____

Step 2: Consider the following things about what you have written: relationships, personal interests, and community. Examine each item in your list to ensure that it still fits.

_____

_____

_____

Step 3: Develop a list of priorities. Identify the most important. Once this is done, review the list and rank them from most to least important. Remove the least important. Re-rank if appropriate. Check for relevance with your earlier list. Eliminate any item that is not relevant.

_____

_____

_____

Step 4: Use the items from the first three steps to develop a personal vision statement. Review and edit the statement as often as needed until you believe it accurately reflects your commitment to more rigorous schools and classrooms.

_____

_____

_____

Tool 25 – Vision Letters

It is also important for teachers and other staff to have a personal vision. The beginning of the school year is a great time to think about vision, but it can take place at any time. A Vision Letter is an engaging and motivating way for teachers to share their visions of their classrooms.

Ask teachers to imagine that it is the last day of school. This year turned out to be their best year ever, one that far exceeded their expectations. Now, ask them to write a letter or e-mail addressed to another teacher describing the past year—all that students accomplished, the rigor of their classroom, ways they supported student learning. Next, ask the teachers to share their letters with a colleague. Use this as a starting point to discuss the shared vision of the school.

Another alternative is to ask teachers to write the letter to you, including all the elements described above. However, also ask them to describe how you helped them accomplish their goals. You can then use the letter as a part of a conversation with each teacher about his or her vision of a more rigorous classroom and how it relates to your vision of a more rigorous school. It also provides an opportunity for you to understand how you can help each teacher accomplish his or her goals.

What if...

"Our faculty loved the vision letter activity. It energized them to think about having the best year ever. I am also better connected with them, since I understand their visions for their classrooms. How can I keep the momentum going?"

Use the vision letter throughout the year. When you meet with teachers to talk about their work, reference the letter and ask about their progress. Inquire about any support they may need to make their vision a reality. Are there barriers you can remove for their success? You'll want to reinforce the idea that writing the letter was not a "one-time" activity, but something to be used to guide teacher work throughout the year. One principal we worked with had people review their vision letter in the middle of the year and again at the end. The vision letter was a vehicle to get teachers to continue to think about improving rigor throughout the year.

Tool 26 – The Hot Air Balloon

It is essential that teachers and leaders possess a clear and compelling personal vision, but personal vision alone is not sufficient. Effective leaders recognize the importance of working with staff and community to develop, nurture, and sustain a strong, collectively held vision for their more rigorous school.

The "hot-air balloon" is a way to get people talking about vision and thinking about how their school is experienced. Asking participants to consider what they see, what they feel, and what they hear draws on people's senses and makes the vision discussion more relevant.

Tool 26A   Discussion Prompt

Imagine you're hovering in a hot air balloon over your school. It is as rigorous as it might be. What would you see? What would you feel? What would you hear?

You might choose to turn this activity into a two-step process. Draw a simple T-chart similar to the one in Tool 26B-Our View from a Hot Air Balloon. Ask teachers to describe what they would currently see and hear in their school. Then ask them to imagine it is five years in the future; describe what they would see and hear from their hot-air balloon.

Tool 26B   Our View from a Hot Air Balloon

Today	Five Years from Today

Based on the comparison, determine areas of strength that exist in the school. For example, while in today's hot air balloon, teachers see a strong sense of community and collegial atmosphere in the school. They also want that in five years. Next, consider areas for potential growth. This might include characteristics that are not evident at this time, but are desired in five years, such as high expectations for all students.

Tool 26C   Planning from the Hot Air Balloon View

Areas of Strength	Areas for Potential Growth
Next Steps:	

Tool 27 – Create or Recommit to a School-Wide Vision of Rigor

Every school we've worked with has a mission or vision statement. Even the clearest vision statements need occasional review so that the mission and vision are based on up-to-date information about students and their needs. For example, one of the frequent updates is to include an unambiguous statement about the commitment to increasing the rigor of your school. We've found that a review also allows the school community "to recommit to the school's core values and beliefs," one of the things we discussed in Chapter Three: Culture. Tool 27-Process for Developing a School Vision Statement will guide you as you work with your stakeholders to create a vision statement.

Tool 27 Process for Developing a School Vision Statement

Activity 1: What are the things people are pleased with and frustrated about at this school?	
Activity 2: Invite the group to consider the values that should guide the school. You might ask, "As we begin planning for our future, what values are most important to you as we create our vision statement?"	
Activity 3: Ask the group to respond to the following. "Imagine it is the year 2014. We have been able to operationalize our beliefs. What does our school look, sound, and feel like? Describe the vision."	
Activity 4: In work groups, develop a draft mission statement to be shared with the larger group.	
Activity 5: Share the drafts, ask questions, seek clarification, and seek consensus on a statement. Plan to share it with the larger school community for feedback and comment.	

From: Williamson & Blackburn (2009). *The Principalship from A to Z*. Larchmont, NY: Eye on Education.

Tool 28 – Another Approach to Visioning

While the staff in District 102 near Chicago were studying their middle grades program, they created a study group that included teachers, administrators, and parents to participate in the process. The group found that, through their discussion about vision, they developed greater understanding of the varying points-of-view and this understanding helped them reach agreement on a shared vision.

Tool 28   Another Approach to Visioning

Step 1: Discuss current conditions (strengths and opportunities).

Step 2: Use a facilitator to promote participation by everyone in the discussion.

Step 3: Identify focus areas for the vision and provide evidence to support their inclusion.

Step 4: Use technology (a wiki) to invite every member to suggest a statement of vision and supporting objectives; the facilitator can review the statements and synthesize the information for the group.

Step 5: Share all proposed statements of vision with every member, asking for feedback and suggestions.

Step 6: Meet and discuss the proposed vision and each proposed objective, agreeing to keep, merge, or discard based on level of support.

Step 7: Agree on vision and supporting objectives.

Which of these steps would be helpful as you consider creating or revising your school's vision? Which steps would you adjust for your specific situation?

_____

_____

_____

_____

_____

_____

_____

_____

_____

_____

_____

_____

Final Thoughts and Action Planning

A clear vision, and the shared commitment to its success, is one of the most important characteristics of an effective school. It is important to be clear about your own personal vision and to work collaboratively with members of your school community on your shared vision. Working together on your vision builds ownership and commitment, both of which are critical to your work to improve rigor in your school. The Action Plan will help you consider options and next steps.

My Action Plan for Increasing Ownership and Building a Shared Vision

The most important tool from this chapter in my current situation is:

_____

_____

_____

_____

_____

I also think the following concepts and/or tools would be useful in my situation:

_____

_____

_____

_____

_____

I need additional help or resources in the form of:

_____

_____

_____

_____

_____

My next action steps are to:

_____

_____

_____

_____

_____

5

Managing Data

A critical aspect of school reform for today's schools is the ability to effectively manage data. Leaders and teachers are often overwhelmed with the sheer amount of data they have. Many of the schools we work with are unsure how to best use the information. First, let's clarify what we mean by data. Data is all the information you have, or might collect, that you can use to support your efforts to make your school more rigorous. When used correctly, data can be an important tool to guide the decision-making process, measure progress, and monitor accountability.

As you begin this chapter, keep in mind that data is more than test scores. Although scores are one type of data, we will discuss other types, including some new forms you may not use. This doesn't mean you must collect additional data, but you may find that you need alternative data to help you improve rigor in your school. Remember to choose the tools that best suit your needs.

Tools in Chapter Five: Managing Data	
Tool 29	Narrow the Focus
Tool 30	Data Collection
Tool 31	Use an Outside Evaluator
Tool 32	Hold a Focus Group Meeting
Tool 33	Conduct a Student Shadow Study
Tool 34	Instructional Walkthrough
Tool 35	Look at Student Work
Tool 36	Data Source Analysis
Tool 37	Pattern Analysis
Tool 38	Force Field Analysis
Tool 39	Organize a Data Night
Tool 40	Planning Template for Setting Priorities and Goals

We suggest a four-step process when you use data to support your efforts to improve the rigor of your school. We'll describe several tools you can use during each step.

Four Step Approach

Step 1: Be clear about what you want to know
Step 2: Decide how to collect the data
Step 3: Analyze the data
Step 4: Set priorities and goals

Step 1: Be Clear About What You Want to Know

Being clear about what you want to know will help you clarify the data you want to collect and analyze. We suggest that rather than just saying, "We want to increase rigor," you divide the task into smaller, more manageable chunks. For example, you might want to begin with a focus on one part of our definition of rigor (e.g., each student is expected to learn at high levels).

Possible Focus Areas

Expectations for Student Learning

Support for Student Learning

Demonstration of Student Learning

Overall Culture of School Related to Rigor

Tool 29 – Narrow the Focus

We've found that the most successful schools are those in which becoming more rigorous is a journey, rather than an event. They select an initial area for improvement and put energy into it prior to moving to other areas. There are many places you can begin: curriculum, instruction, assessment, or your school's environment.

To help you narrow the focus, in Tool 29A-Sample Characteristics for Expectations of Student Learning, we've identified some characteristics of a rigorous curriculum, rigorous instruction, rigorous assessment, and a school community supportive of rigor. We suggest you introduce these characteristics to your school improvement committee or school leadership team and ask them to help you narrow the focus, where you want to begin and the data that would help to inform your understanding of this area.

TOOL 29A   Sample Characteristics for Expectations of Student Learning

Curriculum	♦ Curriculum reflects new learning for students. ♦ Curriculum is aligned with national and international standards. ♦ Curriculum incorporates higher order thinking skills. ♦ Curriculum focuses on application of knowledge. ♦ Factual, knowledge-based information is applied. ♦ Curriculum offers opportunities for students to see relevance to their own lives and to the real world.
Instruction	♦ Instruction offers opportunities for all students to engage in learning at high levels, demonstrating that all students are expected to answer. ♦ Instruction focuses on higher levels of questioning. ♦ Review of basic information is streamlined and taught in a new manner. ♦ Opportunities for application of learning are incorporated throughout the lesson. ♦ Teacher wait time reflects the belief that all students are expected to answer.
Assessment	♦ Assessment of learning is varied and includes performance-based aspects. ♦ Assessments are structured so that students are given multiple opportunities for success. ♦ Grading reflects a belief that it is mandatory to demonstrate learning.
School Environment	♦ Everyone involved in the school environment encourages students to perform at high levels. ♦ Everyone involved in the school environment models continual learning. ♦ Teachers and other staff support one another's initiatives to improve teaching and learning. ♦ Shared goals focused on student learning are used to assess new ideas and practices.

As you narrow your focus, use the specific characteristics to help you and your stakeholders define and understand the focus area. It may be helpful to describe examples of the characteristics that currently exist in your school using Tool 29B-Focus Area Planning Guide.

Tool 29B   Focus Area Planning Guide

Overall Area of Focus:		
Specific Characteristics to Assess	Current Examples (Ways We Think We Meet This)	Items to Consider

What if...

"We began to discuss narrowing our focus, but we really need to address all areas. We couldn't figure out where to begin, and everyone left the meeting totally overwhelmed. What do I do next?"

Be really clear that you intend to focus on one area. Occasionally, the perception is that everything must be addressed immediately. You could talk with your leadership team, or school improvement team about setting priorities and selecting a focus area. One principal we worked with asked the leadership team to rank the areas and make a recommendation to the faculty. It may also be important for you, as a leader, to give your stakeholders permission to narrow their focus. At the same time, you will want to be clear that each of the areas will be addressed at some point in time.

Step 2: Decide How to Collect Data

A: Determine the Data You Need

After you've determined a focus area, you will want to think about the data you already have available. Most schools routinely gather data. Think about what you already have and how it might be used to guide your work.

Examples of Frequently Available Data

◆ Student grades or test scores

◆ Student, parent, and staff surveys

◆ School climate data

◆ Curriculum audit results

◆ Audit of rigor by an external expert

◆ Report of alignment with state or national standards

You will probably find some of these data helpful. But you may also find that you need additional, more targeted data to give you the information needed to support your work. You probably have demographic data about your students and you probably have data about student achievement and learning. You may want more information about the instructional activities in your classrooms or information about the perceptions of students and families. Reflect for a moment about your data.

Possible Existing Data:

_____

_____

_____

_____

_____

Possible Additional Data Needed:

_____

_____

_____

_____

_____

It may be helpful to phrase your issue as a question. For example, "Do we have high expectations for each student in our building?" "Do we provide appropriate support for each student in our building?" What is your focus area? How can you turn it into a question?

Focus Issue:

_____

_____

_____

_____

_____

Turn It Into A Question:

_____

_____

_____

_____

_____

Then, consider what data you already have, and what types of data you would like to collect. Again, you likely have data readily available to you. Determine the complementary data you need to form a more complete picture of your school's efforts to improve rigor.

There are different types of data, but generally they fall into four categories: demographic data, student achievement and learning data, instructional process data, and attitudinal data.

Types of Data

Demographic Data: These data describe the students and is most often used to understand the student learning data. It provides insight into equity within your student learning data. Demographic data will reveal "who got it."

Achievement and Learning Data: This is data that tells us what is going on in a school or district. It tells us what students learned, what they achieved. These data help us understand how students are achieving. Student learning data will reveal "what students got."

Instructional Process Data: This is the data that helps you understand why students achieved at the level that they did. If student achievement in mathematics is low, you might look at the type of mathematics that students do, the time they spend on math, or the alignment of mathematics with state and local standards or benchmarks. School process data will reveal "how or why they got it."

Attitudinal Data: These data tell you about how people feel about a program, about how they experience your school or district program. Attitudinal or perception data will reveal, "how they feel or what they believe about it."

From: Williamson & Blackburn (2009). *The Principalship from A to Z.*

Tool 30 – Data Collection

Because you can be overwhelmed by all of the data that is available, we've found it helpful to use a chart to organize what you have and what you need. As we mentioned earlier, we find it useful to organize data collection around a specific question or issue. Tool 30A-Sample Data Collection focuses on the belief that all students can learn at high levels.

As you will see on page 74, we've included samples of data that typically exists in schools, such as specific demographic data, test scores, and grades. In the third column, you will see additional data that can be helpful, but is not as commonly available. Keep in mind these are just examples for your review before you create your own plan.

Tool 30A   Sample Data Collection

Question/Issue: Does the instruction at _____ School reflect a belief that all students can learn at high levels?		
Data Type	**Available Existing Data**	**Data to Collect**
Demographic Data	Gender Ethnicity Attendance Socio-Economic Status Retention Rates Second Language Learners Students with Special Needs	Student mobility Feeder school attended
Student Achievement and Learning Data	Scores on state achievement tests Grades Diagnostic Test Scores	Disaggregate based on gender, ethnicity, and socio-economic status Gather test-item analysis data and disaggregate
Instructional Process Data	Classroom response opportunities Walkthrough data	Conduct a shadow study of students Disaggregate student achievement data with teachers' participation in professional development on new reading program
Attitudinal and Perception Data	School climate surveys Focus group interviews Teacher Surveys	Conduct parent climate survey

Consider the samples given in the above chart. What is your focus area related to rigor? Now, think of the data we listed. Which apply in your specific situation? What other data do you currently have? What did we suggest that might help you assess your situation? Use Tool 30B-Collect Your Data to detail the data for your focus area.

TOOL 30B Collect Your Data

Question/Issue:		
Data Type	**Available Existing Data**	**Data to Collect**
Demographic Data		
Student Achievement and Learning Data		
Instructional Process Data		
Attitudinal and Perception Data		

B: Decide How You Will Collect Data

There are lots of different ways to collect data. We believe it is helpful to have a mix of quantitative measures and qualitative measures. For example, student grades and test scores might be complemented by open-ended surveys or focus group conversations.

We'll look at several tools for collecting data, including the use of a rubric with an outside evaluator, holding focus group sessions, organizing an instructional walkthrough, looking at student work, and shadowing students.

Tool 31 – Use an Outside Evaluator

In Chapter Two: Rigor, Research, and the Change Process, we introduced the concept of using a rubric for self-evaluation. Rubrics are often used solely for internal assessments, but these are often inflated, may not accurately reflect what is really going on, or lack credibility with parents and other external groups.

Another way to use a rubric is to have someone knowledgeable in rigorous schools and classrooms conduct an assessment. They can use an established rubric to measure your school's current status and progress at becoming more rigorous. Assessments conducted by experts, external to the school, frequently have much greater credibility and can help to identify a school improvement agenda. Tool 31B-Working with an External Evaluator can be used to guide your work with an outside evaluator.

What if...

"Our district hired someone to evaluate our schools a few years ago. Even though some of the suggestions were helpful, it was a negative experience for our faculty. I'm just not sure I want to go through that again."

It's important to realize that anytime you ask someone to evaluate your school, the purpose is improvement. We recommend involving all stakeholders in advance and focusing on the goal. In order to improve, you need an outside perspective on areas of growth. It's likely that your teachers already know their strengths, and just as we do with students, the evaluation will focus on the areas where there is room for progress. Also, be sure to let a new evaluator know what happened in the past, and work with him or her to present the information in a positive way. Finally, after the visit, allow for reflection, then guide stakeholders toward next steps for addressing the recommendations.

Tool 31A   Tips for Using an Outside Evaluator

Choose the Right Evaluator

- Choose an evaluator who is credible in the area of rigor.

- Ensure their perspective of rigor matches your vision. Do some research, talk with potential evaluators, and be sure that they are focused on the things included in your vision. For example, you might not want someone focused primarily on adding advanced placement classes.

Prepare for the Visit

- Determine the focus for the visit, as well as the types of data collection (walkthroughs, focus groups, etc.).

- Prior to the visit, ensure the evaluator has an understanding of the school's demographics, mission and vision, history, and current initiatives.

- Send all requested information, including data about your school, your school improvement plan, student learning data, and demographics. Provide this in the format preferred by the evaluator (electronic and/or print).

- Discuss the upcoming visit with teachers, leaders, and all involved stakeholders. Ensure everyone understands the purpose of the visit, as well as planned activities.

- Prepare multiple copies of all assessment tools for the evaluator.

- Prepare a map and suggested schedule for the evaluator.

- Prepare a room or area for the evaluator to use during the visit. Ideally, this provides privacy for the evaluator.

During the Visit

- Meet the evaluator to ensure they have all needed materials.

- Facilitate as needed, but also give the evaluator space to do his or her job.

- Don't ask for conclusions early in the process; give the evaluator time to complete the data-gathering process and reflect for analysis.

After the Visit

- Take time to reflect on the recommendations.

- Discuss the recommendations with your stakeholders. Begin by reinforcing the purpose of the visit, as well as how it matches the vision and goals set by the entire team.

- Work with your leadership team and/or all stakeholders to develop a plan for implementing the recommended actions.

NOTE: The term evaluator refers to an evaluator and his or her team.

Tool 31B   Working with an External Evaluator

Selecting the Evaluator:

_____ Identify potential evaluators and their work in the area of rigor.

_____ Gather information about potential evaluators to assure their vision of rigor aligns with your vision and that of your district.

Preparing for the Visit:

_____ Determine focus for initial visit including data to be collected.

_____ Provide evaluator with information about school's demographics, mission and vision, history, and current improvement efforts.

_____ Send agreed upon information to evaluator so that they can read and prepare for the visit.

_____ Talk with teachers, leaders, and other stakeholders about the visit, its purpose, and what will occur during the visit.

_____ Prepare a sufficient number of assessment tools for the evaluator's use.

_____ Have a map of the school and a suggested schedule prepared.

_____ Identify the room or area that the evaluator will use during the visit assuring that the evaluator has privacy for their work.

During the Visit:

_____ Arrange to meet the evaluator and assure that they have needed information and materials.

_____ Provide the evaluator with space to do his or her work, but be available to facilitate as needed.

_____ Allow the evaluator to complete their data gathering and provide time to reflect on the data before you ask for any observations or conclusions.

_____ Be clear about when observations and conclusions will be shared and when any agreed upon reports will be prepared.

Following the Visit:

_____ Take time to reflect on the observations, conclusions, and recommendations.

_____ Share and discuss the observations and recommendations with stakeholders. Be sure and reinforce the purpose of the visit, as well as how the visit aligned with the vision and goals set by the team.

_____ Work with your leadership team and stakeholders to develop a plan to address the issues in the recommendations.

NOTE: The term evaluator refers to an evaluator and his or her team.

Tool 32 – Hold a Focus Group Meeting

A focus group is a group of individuals brought together to participate in a guided discussion about an issue of interest. Focus group sessions consist of structured discussion and are generally most useful when conducted by an outside facilitator. This encourages participants to speak more freely, especially about difficult issues. The information that emerges should be scripted, analyzed for patterns and themes, and publicly shared and discussed. A focus group can help you understand how people experience your school.

When you arrange for a focus group, be clear about the purpose of the meeting. Most often, the purpose is to understand stakeholder needs and to gather data about the current status of the school or a specific program related to rigor. Explain that data will not be identified with an individual and that only themes will be reported, which allows for limited individual confidentiality. Prior to the meeting, develop and use a set of guiding questions to start the discussion. Finally, always follow up responses with requests for more detail and information. It is usually helpful to ask for an example that illustrates the thinking. Tool 32-Examples of Guiding Questions or Probes for Focus Groups can facilitate your focus group meeting.

Tool 32   Examples of Guiding Questions or Probes for Focus Groups

General:

- ◆ Talk with me about our school. What's most important for me to know?
- ◆ What are our school's strengths? It's challenges?
- ◆ Describe your experience with this school.
- ◆ What qualities define a successful _____ school?
- ◆ Discuss this school's curriculum.

Specific:

- ◆ Talk about classroom activities that you would describe as rigorous. What was going on? Why was it rigorous?
- ◆ When you feel really supported in your learning (or your student feels supported in his/her learning), what is happening?
- ◆ How would you describe the rigor of this school's curriculum? What are examples of a rigorous classroom experience?
- ◆ Discuss the expectations teachers have for student learning.
- ◆ What suggestions do you have for strengthening our instruction to assure a more rigorous experience for students?
- ◆ If you could change one thing at this school, what would it be? Please explain.

Other Questions You Would Like to Ask:

What if...

"We wanted to do a focus group of parents. First, it was difficult to get parents to come in. The ones who came are the ones who come to everything. Then, one or two of them dominated the conversation. By the end, we didn't have any new information at all, just that they liked the school."

Before you schedule a focus group meeting with parents, you may want to talk with several, representing the diversity of your student population, about the activity. Some parents are reluctant to meet at school because they did not experience success in school. Others are reluctant because they worry about any retaliation that might occur. Still others have language and cultural barriers to participating in such a group. A leader in Connecticut worked with a local parish priest to host the meeting. She also had a translator present to facilitate communication with her parents from Puerto Rico. Another school in Michigan held the meetings in a local community center or library.

To avoid a handful of parents dominating the discussion, you will want to develop a plan for the meeting. Parents can meet in small groups and then report their discussion or you could use a modified jigsaw activity.

Finally, parents are more likely to come to school when there is some activity involving their children. Some principals arrange focus group meetings in conjunction with parent conferences, music performances, or on activity nights. Others provide child care during the meetings. Generally, you'll have more participation if you consider the parents' schedule and other commitments.

Tool 33 – Conduct a Student Shadow Study

A different way to gather information about the instructional experience of students is to conduct a shadow study. Shadow studies involve selecting students at random and "shadowing" them throughout their day.

The protocol, originally developed by NASSP (Lounsbury & Johnston, 1985), charts the experience of students every five-to-seven minutes. This allows the observer to show the ebb and flow of activities during the day. Spending the entire day with a student and documenting their experience using Tool 33A-Shadow Study Observation Form provides interesting insights into the student experience. Of course, students quickly figure out that something is going on. The best approach is to talk with the student and assure them that you are not gathering information about them to report to the office.

Tool 33A   Shadow Study Observation Form

Time	Specific Behavior At 5–7 Minute Intervals	Comments / Impressions

At the end of the day, spend some time with the student you shadowed. Ask him or her about the day and about his or her typical experiences. Provide time for him or her to tell you about what school is like.

Tool 33B   End of Day Questions

- ♦ If a new student moved in next door to you, what are three good things about this school that you would tell her or him?
- ♦ What are some things about the school that you would change if you could?
- ♦ How do you feel, in general, about your classes? Do they challenge you?
- ♦ How do you feel, in general, about your teachers? Do they provide enough support for you to be successful?
- ♦ What did you learn today? How do you think that learning is useful?

What if...

"I like the idea of a shadow study, but I don't have a full day to do it. Will it work with less time? Also, I wonder if it might work better if I swapped schools with another principal since the student wouldn't know me."

There are many ways to conduct a shadow study. You can use part of a day to do the shadowing or you might spread it out over two days. Occasionally, people are reluctant to shadow students from their own school because they are gathering information about their colleagues. In some districts schools are paired so that you shadow students in a neighboring school and teachers and principals at that school shadow your students. Remember you want the data to help inform your improvement. You may get better data if the shadow study is conducted by people who don't work in your school.

Tool 34 – Instructional Walkthrough

An instructional walkthrough provides yet another way to collect data. We do not suggest a quick tour of the school but rather a focused visit to your school's instructional areas to collect information about your school's program.

Walkthroughs should always be designed and implemented in a collaborative way. When that happens, the walkthrough can be a useful tool to gather information about the rigor of your school's program. There are three stages in a successful walkthrough: Prior to conducting the walkthrough, conducting the walkthrough, and following the walkthrough.

Tool 34A   Prior to Conducting the Walkthrough

____ Work with your teachers to be clear about the purpose of the walkthrough. You might use it to see how information from a recent workshop is being used or to look for the presence of a single indicator of rigor.

____ Inform and prepare teachers. They need to know who will be visiting, what data will be collected, and how the data will be shared and used following the walkthrough.

____ Encourage teachers to conduct classes as they normally would, essentially ignoring the visitors and not interrupting routines. This is very important because a successful walkthrough collects data about current programs and practices. A walkthrough should never be a special event with specially designed lessons or activities.

____ Develop a plan for how observers will move throughout the school. You'll want observers to visit all instructional settings, not focus on just one area of the school. It may be appropriate to observe on more than one day and/or at various times throughout the day in the same classroom or instructional area.

____ Identify the time needed to observe. Determine the amount of time that observers will observe each setting. The longer an observer stays in a classroom, the more likely the visit is to change instruction.

Conducting the Walkthrough

Encourage observers to visit all instructional settings. Focus on the instructional practices present during the first few minutes of an observation. Data are recorded based on these initial observations.

Observers may want to talk with students. Responses from students can provide helpful information about your instructional program and expectations for students.

Tool 34B   Possible Questions for Students

♦ What are you learning?

♦ Why do you need to know this information?

♦ What did you learn previously that helped you with this lesson?

♦ How do you know your work is good enough?

♦ If you want to make your work better, how do you know what to improve?

♦ What is an example of something you've done where you had to work hard but also learned a lot?

After observers make their observations, they should move from the setting to a place of privacy and discreetly record the information. Assure that the recording of each observation is anonymous. Observers want to get a view of instructional practice across the school, not in any particular classroom.

Following the Walkthrough

What you do after the walkthrough is just as important as what you did during the walkthrough. It is an opportunity to learn about your school and develop a plan for continued improvement.

Tool 34C Following the Walkthrough

_____ Work with your teachers to be clear about the purpose of the walkthrough. You might use it to see how information from a recent workshop is being used or to look for the presence of a single indicator of rigor.

_____ Provide an opportunity for all teachers to study the data and reflect on its meaning. Information that you collect should be available in an open and transparent way, one that invites conversation and discussion. Keeping the data secret only contributes to lack of trust and misunderstanding of the process.

_____ Engage teachers and other school personnel in conversation about the data, patterns that emerge, and how it informs your efforts to improve rigor.

_____ Develop a plan for this collaborative dialogue. Several formats might be considered, including a discussion with the entire faculty, talking with a team, or the faculty at one grade level or in one content area or meeting with your school improvement team.

What if...

"When I mention a walkthrough, people just roll their eyes. I'm new this year, and the principal last year did 3 minute walkthroughs, but then used them for individual teacher evaluations. I thought the purpose was to understand the overall school, not focus on one teacher. How do I help my teachers understand how I want to use walkthroughs without criticizing the former principal?"

We don't think walkthroughs should ever be used to evaluate teachers since they provide only a snapshot of what is going on at one point in time. To overcome the legacy of your predecessor, you may want to work with your school improvement team to develop a process. Be sure to include teachers in the walkthroughs and to share the information you gain in a very public way while maintaining confidentiality of individual teachers. At a middle school in Los Angeles, teachers conducted the walkthroughs and posted the information on a large chart in the faculty lounge. They did not identify individual teachers. The emphasis was on looking for patterns and seeing improvement over time.

Tool 35 – Look at Student Work

Finally, don't forget that a powerful source of information is student work. You might conduct a walkthrough with faculty to observe the school and student work or examine student work during grade-level, team, or department meetings. Tools for this concept are found in Chapter Six: Professional Development, but there are several different protocols for looking at student work. They are available at the Looking at Student Work website sponsored by the Annenberg Institute for School Reform http://www.lasw.org.

Step 3: Analyze the Data

Be sure to involve your school improvement team or other shared governance group in the process of analyzing the data. We've always found it helps to have people with many different points-of-view look at data. Always keep an open mind, rather than pre-determining the results. Otherwise, you may not see the full picture. First, analyze the information provided by each data source.

Tool 36 – Data Source Analysis

One of the most helpful things you can do when analyzing your data is to identify strengths and areas for potential growth. You may find that you need even more information.

Using Tool 36-Data Source Analysis, talk with your shared governance group about the data and work together to identify strengths and opportunities. Use one form for each data source.

What if...

"After we collected data and analyzed it, there just seems to be so much! Some data indicate one area, another data source indicated something else. What now?"

You'll want to look at your varied data and conduct an analysis to see if any patterns emerge. Occasionally, you will see similar or related issues appear across data sources. This is a task best done with a small group, perhaps your school improvement team. Different people will have different perspectives and see different things in the data. Remember that it is wise to focus your energy on one area rather than dissipate your efforts across many different topics.

Tool 36   Data Source Analysis

Data Source:

Areas of Strength	Areas for Potential Growth	Areas that Need More Information

Tool 37 – Pattern Analysis

One thing you will want to do is look for patterns across multiple sources of data. This will prove helpful when you begin to prioritize action steps in areas that need the most work. You may find that you don't have enough data to select an area of focus. If so, consider how you might gather additional data. Once you have looked at individual data sources, use Tool 37-Pattern Analysis to assess patterns.

What if...

"We've already spent hours and hours breaking down our diagnostic test data, and we have reports from our district on standardized test scores. We're tired of analyzing data. Why should I use a pattern analysis?"

We understand that many leaders and teachers are tired. But we also see that one of the major problems related to data is conflicting information. As one teacher-leader commented in a recent work-shop, "The state test tells me one thing, our district tests tell me something else, and I see the student everyday and observe other strengths and weaknesses. If none of the data agrees, then what's the point?" Although this may be an extreme example, it is true that different data can produce different results. That is why a pattern analysis is critical. Simply take the analysis you have already completed, and begin to compare it. Look for those patterns that occur across the data points. Then, as you look for specific areas for improvement, begin with those that are identified from multiple sources. The pattern analysis is also helpful to highlight areas where you may need more data to make an informed decision.

First, you will identify strengths and weaknesses for each data source. Then, look for areas identified by more than one data source. This will allow you to identify patterns.

Tool 37 Pattern Analysis

Data Source	Strengths	Areas for Growth

Overall Areas of Focus (based on multiple data sources)	
Strengths	**Areas for Growth**

Focus Your Efforts

Many schools try to work on too many things at the same time. This dilutes the energy of teachers and administrators and may detract from your ability to make progress on any one area. A thorough look at the data will help you prioritize areas for improvement. It is essential to involve your teachers in this process but you may also want to involve families and other stakeholder groups.

Plan thoughtfully and purposefully for this discussion. One of the lessons we've learned is the importance of presenting data in a non-threatening way. We've never worked in a school where people purposely tried to harm students. So we always focus on areas for growth, rather than areas of concern; opportunities rather than weaknesses.

Suggested Words and Phrases for Discussing Data

As you look at the data, what patterns do you see?

What do the data say are our strengths, our points of pride?

What do the data indicate are some opportunities for improvement? How might we select a priority?

What other data might we want to collect so that we can more completely understand the issues?

Tool 38 – Force Field Analysis

A Force Field Analysis is a tool for diagnosing issues and it can provide clear guidelines for action. The process works well with small as well as large groups and provides an opportunity to examine both facilitators and inhibitors of change.

When you use a Force Field Analysis, you consider both driving forces and restraining forces. Driving forces are those forces that affect an issue and are pushing in a particular direction; they tend to be things that initiate a change and keep it going. Restraining forces are forces acting to restrain or decrease the driving forces.

Tool 38A Sample Forces

Sample Driving Forces	Sample Restraining Forces
Data about student learning	Belief that some students can't achieve at high levels
Demographic data	
Number of students who drop out of college after graduating from your high school	Pressure from parents for students to make all A's
Data from local employers about numbers of new employees who need basic retraining	Apathy
	Contractual issues
	Costs of an innovation

Using the Force Field Analysis

As you work to increase the rigor in your school, a force field analysis will allow you to look at all the forces for or against your initiative. It helps you to plan for or reduce the impact of the opposing forces, and strengthen and reinforce the supporting forces. Tool 38B-Force Field Analysis Form, will guide you through the process.

When conducting a force field analysis, state the problem or desired state in clear, concrete terms. Next, discuss and identify the factors that are working for and against the desired state.

Then, review and clarify each factor. Once you agree on the list of factors, determine the strength of each factor. For example, assign a score to each force, from 1 (weak) to 5 (strong) or high, medium or low. Finally, discuss the factors and their scores. This will help you identify appropriate next steps. Those factors working against the desired state may become the focus of plans of action. This information will help you set your priorities and goals.

What if...

"I'm not sure what you mean by factors working for or against the desired state. Does that mean the people who will or won't support the initiative?"

Certainly you may consider specific people as factors who will work for or against increasing rigor in your school. Listing specific people in the columns, though, should only be the first step. Reflect on your situation at a deeper level. For example, factors working against your efforts may include: resistance due to the large number of changes that have been made in the school over the last year, instructional apathy due to concerns over school discipline, or fear from parents that students will lose college scholarships if grades are lowered due to increased rigor.

A force field analysis allows you and your stakeholders to air all issues that can help propel the initiative forward, or might derail it. Don't limit your discussion to isolated people, be sure to look at the broader issues.

Tool 38B   Force Field Analysis Form

Description of Problem or Desired State:			
Factors Working For	**Ranking**	**Factors Working Against**	**Ranking**

Goals and Next Steps:

Tool 39 – Organize a Data Night

Recently, Ron was working with a school near Chicago to look at their data and develop an improvement plan. A task force of teachers, parents, and administrators was created to conduct the review. The group revised the school's vision and then identified more than twenty different sources of data that could be used to help identify action steps. Everyone received a notebook filled with the data. A wiki was also developed so that task force members could share their observations as they reviewed the data.

The task force held several different "data nights" where they met, worked together to examine the data, discuss its implications, and rate the school's current success in the area. Small work groups met to continue the analysis and suggest action steps.

These data nights were helpful because they assured that everyone had the same data, had an opportunity to talk about its meaning, and to contribute to the analysis. These meetings helped the group move forward to develop a plan that would support the continued improvement of the program.

Tool 39   Organize a Data Night

Prior to Data Night	During Data Night	After Data Night
◆ Decide who to involve ◆ Be clear about data to be gathered and how it is to be shared with the group ◆ Identify a process for looking at and analyzing the data ◆ Consider using a facilitator who's role is to help the group conduct the analysis ◆ Agree on norms for the discussion and interaction	◆ Arrange the room to facilitate discussion ◆ Organize the group to promote interaction and different points-of-view ◆ Review agreed upon norms of collaboration ◆ Assure that everyone has a copy of the data ◆ Follow your plan rather than jump from topic to topic ◆ Be diligent about maintaining a group memory by recording information about the analysis and additional questions that emerge ◆ Be clear about what should be shared and with whom	◆ Share the minutes and/or analysis with members ◆ Distribute information based on what the group agreed to share ◆ Plan additional meetings to talk further about the data or your findings ◆ Use the analysis to guide decision-making and set priorities

Step 4: Set Priorities and Goals

The fourth step is to work with your school improvement team or other collaborative group to determine priorities based on your area of focus and the data analysis. Tool 40-Planning Template for Setting Priorities and Goals may facilitate your discussion.

Once you determine your priorities, goals, or area of focus, study and select strategies that will allow you to address the area of focus. This is a pivotal point. Too often, we gather and analyze data, set goals, but then do not use that information to make decisions on an ongoing basis.

Using your Pattern Analysis (Tool 37), note the data sources you used. Next, identify the area for potential growth, such as incorporating more activities in which each student is required to demonstrate learning. Third, design a specific way to track success. How will everyone know if they are making progress toward the goal? What does success look like? Finally, detail the specific action steps that are needed to accomplish the goal.

Tool 40 Planning Template for Setting Priorities and Goals

Data Source(s)		
Area for Potential Growth	**Indicators for Measuring Success**	**Action Steps**

Final Thoughts and Action Planning

Using data to guide your efforts to improve the rigor of your school is important, but be cautious about simply gathering data. The most important activity is conducting a thoughtful analysis of the data so it can guide selection of school improvement strategies.

The most successful leaders are those who routinely use data to guide their work. They recognize the importance of using a balanced set of data sources and student achievement scores, as well as information about instructional practices and student and family perceptions. They are comfortable with data and recognize the power of data to help improve their school. Using the Action Plan, what are your next steps?

My Action Plan for Managing Data

The most important tool from this chapter in my current situation is:

_____

_____

_____

_____

_____

_____

_____

I also think the following concepts and/or tools would be useful in my situation:

_____

_____

_____

_____

_____

_____

_____

_____

I need additional help or resources in the form of:

_____

_____

_____

_____

_____

_____

_____

My next action steps are to:

_____

_____

_____

_____

_____

_____

_____

6

Professional Development

Effective professional development is an essential part of your effort to improve rigor. Traditionally, professional development has included workshops, seminars, courses, or conferences. These types of activities have varied in terms of effectiveness, and contemporary professional development adds to these choices with a wider range of activities.

Contemporary professional development includes peer coaching, collaborative work teams, study groups, action research teams, mentoring, and other activities that support a teacher-leadership approach.

Tools in Chapter Six: Professional Development	
Tool 41	Assess Your Professional Development Efforts
Tool 42	Refining Your Professional Development
Tool 43	Professional Learning Communities: Assess Your Own Dispositions
Tool 44	Book Study
Tool 45	Looking at Student Work
Tool 46	Learning Walks
Tool 47	Lesson Studies
Tool 48	Charrette
Tool 49	Evaluating and Adjusting Curriculum
Tool 50	Aligning Expectations with High Standards
Tool 51	Develop Consistent Expectations
Tool 52	Choosing a Strategy
Tool 53	PRESS Forward Model for Action Planning

Contemporary Professional Development

According to the National Staff Development Council (www.learningforward.org), contemporary professional development should have three characteristics:

1. Results Driven

2. Standards-Based

3. Job Embedded

Professional development should focus on clear results and promote the growth and learning of teachers and administrators. Activities should be based on standards, and they should be thoroughly woven into the job, rather than simply being an activity that is done as an "extra," possibly outside of work hours or on staff development days.

Lessons from Award-Winning Schools

Barbara's research examining staff development in schools that won the U. S. Department of Education's Award for Staff Development (Blackburn, 2000) identified several characteristics. Effective staff development had a clear purpose linked to research, student data, and goals. Teachers were accountable for using the professional development in their classrooms to impact student learning. There was an emphasis on developing a common, shared language to talk about issues. Decisions about professional development were made with teacher input and professional development incorporated relevant, practical, hands-on activities. Finally, school leaders supported professional development and it took place in a positive, collegial atmosphere. Using Tool 41-Assess Your Professional Development Efforts, reflect on your current professional development.

TOOL 41   Assess Your Professional Development Efforts

Rate the status of your professional development using this scale:
 	
    1 – Needs More Work   3 – Underway but still working on it
    2 – Getting Started   4 – Doing Very Well
	Rating

1. Our professional development is guided by a clear purpose linked to research, data about student learning, and clearly identified goals and needs.	
2. Following professional development, we're held accountable for using the things we've learned in our classrooms to impact student learning.	
3. We're developing a common, shared language.	
4. Decision-making about professional development includes teacher input.	
5. Our professional development incorporates relevant, practical, hands-on activities.	
6. We integrate initial professional development with opportunities for follow-up and application.	
7. Our leaders support professional development and it occurs in a positive, collegial atmosphere.	
8. We move beyond traditional staff development methods to include options such as inquiry action research projects, book study groups, mentoring, peer coaching, and collaborative work teams.	

How Do These Elements Support Your Efforts Toward Increased Rigor?

Now that you've assessed how you are doing you may want to look more deeply at each of the seven areas using Tool 42-Refining Your Professional Development.

Tool 42   Refining Your Professional Development

Area	Strengths	Opportunities
Clear purpose: What area of rigor do we want to improve? Is it justified by the data? Does the research support the plan?		
Accountability: How will the PD be used in the classroom? How will you know students benefit? What will you see in classrooms?		
Common, shared language: How will you work to develop and use a shared language to talk about your work?		
Shared decision-making: How will teachers be authentically involved in decisions about professional development?		
Relevant, practical, hands-on activities: Are the activities relevant to teachers? Are participants able to interact to increase engagement?		
Opportunity for follow-up and application: How will you incorporate the learning after the training? Does each participant need to develop an action plan? How will you follow-up with teachers?		
Leadership and a positive, collegial atmosphere: Who provides leadership for your professional development plan? How will you use some of your current meeting time for professional development? How will you create a positive, collegial, and supportive atmosphere?		

What if...

"This all sounds good, but some of what we need to do is mandated to us. We don't have a choice. Then what?"

Being told to do things, especially when they may not support your vision of a more rigorous school never feels good. But there are some things you might consider. First, advocate with the district office to allow your school to opt-out of the required activities. It is always helpful to have a specific plan that clearly aligns with your school's vision and your school improvement goals. Second, you might identify a way for people to participate in the required professional development through online activities or through a book study. This approach might minimize the impact and reinforce your focus on collaborative professional development.

Professional Learning Communities

Many schools use professional learning communities as a tool for professional development. The term has become so commonplace it is used to describe almost any sort of collaborative work.

The professional community of learners, originally suggested by Astuto and colleagues (1993) and then promoted by DuFour (2006), reflects the commitment of teachers and administrators who continuously seek to learn and grow professionally and then act on what they learn. The goal is to improve student learning by improving effectiveness. Effective learning communities have three defining characteristics.

Defining Characteristics of PLCs

1. ensuring that students learn

2. a culture of collaboration

3. a focus on results (whatever it takes)

Chapter Nine: Structures that Support Rigor includes a tool (78) you can use to assess the work of your professional learning communities. Here, we've included Tool 43-Professional Learning Communities: Assess Your Own Dispositions that you can use to think about your role as a leader and how you support your professional learning communities.

Tool 43 Professional Learning Communities: Assess Your Own Dispositions

Use this scale to rate your dispositions about professional learning communities:
 	
    1 – Strongly Disagree   3–Agree
    2 – Disagree   4 – Strongly Agree
	Rating

1. I expect the professional staff at this school to use their talents and knowledge to help one another improve as teachers.	
2. I encourage teachers to learn new ideas and use them in the classroom.	
3. It is important to provide time and resources for teachers to do their best work.	
4. I recognize and appreciate good teaching at my school.	
5. I promote honest, open communication among the staff at this school.	
6. As the leader of this school, I ask my teachers to be involved in analyzing student learning data, setting goals, and monitoring our success.	
7. I ask teachers to use a research base to inform our work with students and with one another.	
8. I'm comfortable adopting new practices even if they may not be successful the first time.	
What are the top three areas for improvement for you? What is one step you could take to improve each?	

Collaborative Professional Development Activities

There are many different ways to organize collaborative groups. Like most things, each has advantages and disadvantages. It is important to select a strategy that allows you to maintain momentum on achieving your vision of a more rigorous school, and one that matches the resources you have available.

We want to share five that we've found useful: book study groups, looking at student work, learning walks, lesson study, and use of a charrette. We'll follow with three specific professional development activities related to increasing expectations.

Tool 44 – Book Study

A good way to engage people in their own professional growth is to organize a book study group. At some schools, every teacher is asked to read the same book and work in small groups to discuss the book and its implications for practice. At other schools, teachers may choose from several books and join colleagues who selected the same book for their discussion. Tool 44A-Book Study Protocol contains guidelines for conducting a book study; Tool 44B-Action Plan for a Book Study allows you to design your plan.

TOOL 44A   Book Study Protocol

♦ Membership should be voluntary, but inclusive.

♦ Decide a meeting schedule, meeting place, length of book to be read, and what will happen after the book is read. It is recommended that meetings last no more than one hour and be held at a consistent time and place.

♦ Select a responsible facilitator to keep the group on task and help manage the meetings.

♦ Select a book with a clear objective in mind. For example, use *Rigor is not a Four Letter Word* with teachers to launch the conversation about rigor or use *Rigorous Schools and Classrooms: Leading the Way* with school leaders or your school improvement team.

♦ Conversation is important in a book study. Members of the group share insights, ask questions about the text, and learn from others. It is important to talk about how the ideas can be applied directly in the classroom and how to overcome any potential obstacles.

♦ Journaling is a useful way for members to think about their reading and reflect on how it might be used.

What if...

"Who leads the book study? Is this my responsibility or should teachers lead?"

The choice of a leader depends on your situation. Ideally, you are looking for someone to facilitate discussion. That means they don't need to "teach" a book study session; they need to ask prompting questions and pull the group back together if they get too far off-track. But we have worked with schools where the group dynamics required someone with a stronger, more direct approach. There are also times when an administrator leading the study is a critical part of instructional leadership. Ultimately, you must assess your situation to determine the best approach.

Tool 44B   Action Plan for a Book Study

How will we determine membership?	
What is our meeting schedule?	
Who will be the facilitator?	
What book will we use?	
How will we ensure conversation?	
How will we use journaling?	

Additional information about conducting a book study is available from Eye On Education at http://www.eyeoneducation.com/BookStudyGroupFAQ/BookStudyFAQ.asp.

What if...

"We've tried a book study before and one or two of our teachers dominate the conversation. Often, they try to draw us off track into something else. How can I prevent this or at least lessen the impact?"

This can be a real problem in book study groups or any other collaborative work. There are some things you can do to minimize the impact. First, you might use a pair-share strategy where you pair participants for the discussion. This would lessen the impact on the entire group. Second, you will also want the group to agree on other ground rules. They might include norms about how frequently a person can speak or use of a parking lot to capture the thoughts and ideas without impacting the conversation. Examples of group norms and use of a parking lot are included in Chapter Four of *Rigorous Schools and Classrooms: Leading the Way*.

Tool 45 – Looking at Student Work

A powerful way to improve your school's instructional program is to look at authentic student work. In many schools, teams of teachers, either at the departmental, course, or grade level, examine student work as a way to clarify their own standards for that work, to strengthen common expectations for students, or to align curriculum across faculty.

Because looking at student work significantly alters the norms of a school, it necessitates a climate where faculty are comfortable sharing their work and revealing artifacts about their classroom practice. The Annenberg Institute for School Reform suggests several preliminary steps. Then Tool 45B-Planning for Looking at Student Work gives you an opportunity to plan your activity.

Tool 45A Looking at Student Work Protocol

♦ Talk together about the process and how to ensure it is not evaluative.

♦ Identify ways to gather relevant contextual information (e.g., copy of assignment, scoring guide or rubric).

♦ Select a protocol or guideline for the conversation that promotes discussion and interaction. See www.lasw.org for several different protocols.

♦ Agree on how to select work samples.

♦ Establish a system for providing and receiving feedback that is constructive.

Tool 45B   Planning For Looking at Student Work

What is our process? How can we assure it is not evaluative?	
What materials and resources do we need to collect? Who is responsible for each?	
What protocol or guidelines will we use?	
How will we select work samples?	
What is our system for constructive feedback?	

What if...

"I don't want this to evolve into personal attacks on teachers. How can I prevent that?"

No one wants that to happen and the best way to assure that it doesn't is to agree on the norms and protocol for the discussion. Many examples of a process for looking at student work are available at www.lasw.org. One of our favorites is the "Tuning Protocol" because it has clear guidelines about how to provide feedback about a student work sample. The process of providing both "warm" and "cool" feedback is important. As much as you want to avoid personal attacks, you also want to avoid superficial comments that don't allow the group to learn and grow together.

Another option with groups from a variety of grade levels or schools is to look at the work anonymously. Do not identify the teacher or the school for a particular work sample, as well as using the guidelines we discussed above.

Tool 46 – Learning Walks

A learning walk is a form of instructional walkthrough, but they are typically organized and led by teachers. Learning walks are not evaluative. They are not designed for individual feedback, but instead help participants learn about instruction and identify areas of strength as well as need.

Learning walks provide a "snapshot" of the instructional program at your school. Since participants are in classrooms for only a short time they should not draw conclusions about individual teachers or classes.

One school in Los Angeles held learning walks each month. Groups of teachers conducted the walks looking for evidence of the use of research-based instructional practices described in *Classroom Instruction that Works: Research-Based Strategies for Increasing Student Achievement* (Marzano, Pickering & Pollock, 2001). Another school developed a rubric based on Barbara's three-part definition of rigor (*Rigor is Not a Four-Letter Word*, 2008) and used it to guide their learning walks.

Tool 46-Learning Walks provides guidelines for the learning walk process.

Tool 46   Learning Walks

1. Work with your staff to identify the purpose of the learning walk.

2. Determine the process including length of classroom visits as well as what will occur during the visits. Develop and use a consistent tool for participants to use to record their observations and collect data.

3. Inform staff when the learning walks will occur.

4. Conduct a pre-walk orientation for those participating.

5. Conduct the learning walk and spend no more than 5 minutes in each classroom. Depending on the lesson, talk with the teacher and students, look at student work, and examine the organization of the classroom.

6. Immediately after the walk, ask participants to meet and talk about the information they gathered and how to share it with the faculty. They may develop questions that they would ask to learn more about what is occurring.

7. Develop a plan for sharing the information and for using it to guide your continued school improvement work.

Additional information about conducting a learning walk is available at http://www.swsc.org/16331022110596170/lib/16331022110596170/_files/Learning_Walk_Protocol_2.pdf.

Tool 47 – Lesson Studies

Originally used by Japanese teachers, lesson study emphasizes working in small groups to plan, teach, observe, and critique a lesson. Lesson study involves groups of teachers in a collaborative process designed to systematically examine their practice with the goal of becoming more effective. Tool 47A-Lesson Study Protocol describes the process itself; Tool 47B-Lesson Study Observation is a blank observational form you may want to use or adapt.

Tool 47A   Lesson Study Protocol

♦ Participants should be volunteers but the invitation to participate should be inclusive.

♦ While working on a study lesson, teachers work together to develop a detailed plan for the lesson.

♦ One member of the group teaches the lesson in a real classroom while other members of the group observe the lesson.

♦ The group comes together to discuss their observations about the lesson and student learning.

♦ The group works together to revise the lesson.

♦ Another teacher teaches the revised lesson while group members observe.

♦ The group reconvenes to discuss the observed lesson.

♦ The revision process may continue as long as the group believes it is necessary.

♦ Teachers talk about what the study lesson taught them and how they can apply the learning to their own classroom. They may prepare a report to be shared with others.

Tool 47B Lesson Study Observation

Participant Observer	Date
Grade/Level	Subject
Objective:	

Observations/Notes about Content of Lesson

Observations/Notes about Pacing of Lesson

Observations/Notes about Student Engagement

Other Observations/Notes/Questions

Additional information about conducting a lesson study is available from Teachers College at Columbia University (http://www.tc.columbia.edu/lessonstudy/lesson study.html). The site includes a template for conducting a lesson study and for lesson design (www.tc.columbia.edu/lessonstudy/doc/Lesson_Planning_Tool.pdf).

Tool 48 – Charrette

A "charrette" is a set of agreed upon guidelines for talking with colleagues about an issue. The conversation tends to be more trusting and more substantive because everyone knows the guidelines in advance. Charrettes are often used to improve the work while the work is in progress and are not to be used as an evaluative tool. Tool 48A-Charrette Protocol describes the Charrette process; Tool 48B-Sample Discussion is an excerpt of a typical Charrette discussion. Additional information about the charrette is available at www.turningpts.org/pdf/CharretteProtocol.pdf.

Tool 48A   Charrette Protocol

1. A group or an individual from the group requests a charrette when they want others to help them resolve an issue. Often they are at a "sticking point" and the conversation will help them move forward.

2. Another small group is invited to look at the work and a facilitator is used to moderate the discussion.

3. The requesting group or individual presents its work and states what they need or want from the discussion. The conversation is focused by this presentation.

4. The invited group discusses the issue and the requesting group listens and takes notes. The emphasis is on improving the work, which now belongs to the entire group. "We're in this together" characterizes the discussion.

5. Once the requesting group gets what it needs, it stops the process, summarizes what was learned, thanks participants, and returns to their work.

Adapted From: "Charrette Protocol," written by Kathy Juarez and available on the *Turning Points* website (www.turningpts.org/pdf/CharretteProtocol.pdf).

What if...

"As I look at the samples, I'm not sure about using a Charrette. Due to limited funding, our district closed a school and now I have a mix of teachers who have worked together for years and some teachers who are from the closed school. Will this work?"

The Charrette can be an effective tool for bringing teachers together. The key is point four in the protocol: "The emphasis is on improving the work, which now belongs to the entire group. 'We're in this together' characterizes the discussion." As you begin, you may want to enlist several key teachers from both groups to keep the conversation focused and positive.

TOOL 48B   Sample Discussion

Example of Charrette Discussion

After the group has formed these questions might be used to guide the discussion. Charrettes work best with a facilitator to guide the discussion and monitor the work of the group.

Opening: *Thank you for meeting with me today. We've been asked to get a brief update on the work of the task force looking at providing additional support for students. The group is having difficulty resolving some of the logistical issues related to their recommendations and want our assistance.*

Person/Group Presents Issue: *We have many ideas about how to provide students with additional support both during the school day and beyond. One of the things we haven't resolved is how to assure that teachers will use the strategies and participate in our lunchtime and after school activities.*

Discussion: *Thank you. What questions of clarification does the group have for the task force? Discuss the issue and let's generate several ideas that the task force can use as they continue to work on their recommendations.*

Conclusion: A member of the task force might say, *"Thank you for your suggestions. They helped us clarify the issues and think about the advantages and disadvantages of our plan. We'll continue to work on the issue and share our recommendations with the faculty."*

Tool 49 – Evaluating and Adjusting Curriculum

Central to the effectiveness of professional learning communities is their emphasis on student learning. Built around collaborative endeavors, professional learning communities without a focus on learning fail to achieve all of the potential benefits. The focus must be on student learning, rather than collaboration. Collaborative activity is the tool that enhances a staff's ability to make a difference in the achievement of students.

An important step toward increasing rigor is evaluating the curriculum in your school. Tool 49-Evaluating and Adjusting Curriculum details the four-step process we developed that you can use with teachers to identify adjustments that might be needed to your curriculum. Remember, in a professional learning community, the role of the leader is that of a facilitator, one who guides teachers, but does not force decisions. You may want to group your teachers by subject area and include teachers from a range of grade levels. Including teachers from earlier grade levels and higher grade levels will lead to deeper and more complex discussion.

Tool 49   Evaluating and Adjusting Curriculum

Step 1: Providing Background Knowledge for the Discussion

1. In subject-specific groups, ask teachers to use post-it notes to draft all the topics, concepts, or standards they believe are important. Color-code this by grade level or course (it's easiest to use different colors of post-it notes).

2. Next, compare the notes to your actual state standards. What do teachers include that is not part of your standard? What is missing?

3. Find a set of national standards for comparison (see recommended resources for a starting point). Compare the state standards and the teachers' topic notes to the national standards. What is different?

Step 2: Linking the Research Base

1. Using the information from Chapter One: A Rationale for Rigor in *Rigor is NOT a Four-Letter Word*, discuss the research findings with all teachers. You may want to pull the original research for more information.

2. Ask teachers to compare those findings to what they discovered in their own comparison.

Step 3: Taking the First Step

1. Now, move back into subject-specific groups. Ask teachers to develop a draft outline of content for the year that is aligned with national standards.

2. Sketch out a pacing guide that will allow for **necessary** review, but incorporates more rigorous instruction.

Step 4: Implementation

1. Begin incorporating the new instruction.

2. Ensure appropriate vertical alignment.

3. Meet to discuss what is working, and what needs to be changed.

4. Adjust as needed.

A good way to focus your professional development is to align teacher expectations with state and national standards. Many high-quality rubrics are available for this work. We especially like those from The Southern Regional Education Board (www.sreb.org). They provide detailed descriptions of proficiency with the National Assessment of Education Progress (NAEP) levels for students entering high school.

Tool 50 – Aligning Expectations with High Standards

An informative professional development activity is to look at samples of student work. The purpose is not to evaluative but to align teachers' expectations with standards. The first step is to define high quality in an assignment. Rubrics are an effective way to determine expectations for quality. However, if you don't have a rubric or anything for comparison, you may want to use benchmarks to allow you to frame the conversation through the lens of neutral standards, rather than rely on personal opinions. Tool 50A-Aligning Curriculum with Standards is a sample working template.

Tool 50A   Aligning Curriculum with Standards

Our Priority Topics	State Standards	National Standards

Areas that need more focus:

Areas that need less attention:

Other needed adjustments:

Tool 50B-Making Inferences and Predictions (Reading/Language Arts) is a sample of a rubric developed by the Southern Regional Education Board and available at www.sreb. org. There are many other options you can use; choose the one that best suits your needs.

Tool 50B   Making Inferences and Predictions (Reading/Language Arts)

Basic	Proficient	Advanced
♦ Identify an author's stated position. ♦ Make simple inferences about events and actions that have already occurred, characters' backgrounds, and setting. ♦ Predict the next action in a sequence.	♦ Use evidence from text to infer an author's unstated position. ♦ Identify cause and effect in fiction and nonfiction. ♦ Predict a character's behavior in a new situation, using details from the text. ♦ Formulate an appropriate question about causes or effects of actions.	♦ With evidence from a nonfiction piece, predict an author's viewpoint on a related topic. ♦ Describe the influence of an author's background upon his/her work. ♦ Recognize allusions.

Southern Regional Education Board, 2004.

There are a variety of other sources for standards of all grade levels, including the National Center on Education and the Economy's (NCEE) "New Standards" Performance Standards (www.ncee.org) and the new common, core standards (www.corestandards. org). Choose the national standards that are most helpful for your use.

Tool 51 – Develop Consistent Expectations

While it's helpful to gauge expectations with published standard expectation levels, it's also important to sit down with other teachers and administrators to discuss expectations. Tool 51-Protocol for a Conversation About Expectations is a step-by-step guide to this process.

Tool 51   Protocol for a Conversation About Expectations

Step 1:   Gather copies of a standard assignment, such as a short essay, completed by students. Be sure to have copies from several teachers.

Step 2:   Share copies of the assignment with the group and ask everyone to assess it.

Step 3:   Meet to discuss the results. Use prompts to guide the discussion. For example, "How do you determine quality?," "What do you consider in a quality assignment?," or "What do you expect students to know in order to complete this assignment?"

Step 4:   You may want to extend the conversation to other grade levels. Discussion prompts might include, "What are some areas that students struggle with?" or "What do you expect students to know before they come into your class?"

What if...

"We tried to do some vertical alignment activities earlier in the year. They were a disaster, to say the least. My teachers don't want other teachers telling them what to teach!"

The work should never be about telling someone else what to teach. It is important to structure these discussions so that both teachers contribute to the discussion and shape decisions. Rather than relying on individual preferences, use state or national standards, and the district's curriculum guide, to organize the work. Every district will approach the work differently, but some schools we've worked with are clear that a certain percentage of instruction must follow the curriculum and pacing guides and the remainder can be at the discretion of the teacher. That allows teachers to continue some of their unique instructional activities.

Selecting an Appropriate Strategy

Now that you've had an opportunity to learn about these seven strategies, use Tool 52-Choosing a Strategy to think about how each strategy could be used at your school to impact student learning.

Tool 52 Choosing a Strategy

Strategy	How this strategy could impact student learning
Book Study Groups: Use a book such as *Rigor is Not a Four Letter Word* for small groups to talk about increasing rigor in your school.	
Looking at Student Work: Teams of teachers look at samples of student work to align expectations and promote quality. (www.lasw.org)	
Learning Walks: Similar to walkthroughs, learning walks are led by teachers and designed to gather data about instructional practices.	

(continued)

Strategy	How this strategy could impact student learning
Lesson Study: Small groups of teachers work together to design, teach, and refine a lesson with the focus on improved student learning. (http://www.tc.edu/lessonstudy/lessonstudy.html)	
A Charrette: A protocol for a conversation. Usually a teacher requests the thinking of others as a way to support their work or when experiencing a difficulty with work.	
Evaluating and Adjusting Curriculum: A series of professional development activities to discuss and compare your current standards and expectations with other recognized standards.	
Aligning Expectations with High Standards: An alternative way to look at curriculum and instruction, this activity involves looking at samples of student work and comparing them to standard expectations.	
A Conversation About Expectations: A guide to facilitating discussions of expectations; especially useful for vertical alignment.	

What if...

"It seems like for several of these that teachers must be open to honestly discussing their practice and seeking feedback. I'm not sure our teachers are willing to do that."

All of these approaches rely on the goodwill of participants. Before you adopt any of the approaches it is important to talk about the norms to be used for the conversation. We've worked with lots of groups and really like the Seven Norms of Collaboration developed by Garmston and Wellman (www.adaptiveschools.com). These norms focus on creating a culture of inquiry where every participant feels it is safe to participate.

Tool 53 – PRESS Forward Model for Action Planning

All of the strategies we've shared can make a positive difference in your school. You will need to determine which ones may be most effective in your situation, and you'll likely need to customize them to your setting. For example, for the curriculum alignment activity, high school teachers tend to meet in departments, middle schools in teams, and elementary schools by grade levels. However, it is critical to start with a plan that incorporates the elements of effective professional development: focused on results, job embedded, and standards based.

We've developed Tool 53A-PRESS Forward Model for Planning Professional Development. You design a plan that has a clear purpose, is related and connected to other aspects of your school community, has a set of clear outcomes and action steps, and describes the support that is needed to be successful.

Our plan is cyclical, with benchmarks built into each stage of the process so that you can reflect on your successes and refine your plan before you move forward. Tool 53B-Template for PRESS Forward provides a blank form for your use.

TOOL 53A PRESS Forward Model for Planning Professional Development

PRESS Forward	
Purpose	Why are we doing professional development on rigor?
Relationships and Connections	How does a focus on rigor relate to our mission, our goals, and the needs of our students? How does it connect with other initiatives in our school?
Expected Outcomes	If the professional development is effected, what changes will we see related to teachers' practice and student learning?
Steps to Take	What are the specific action steps we need to take to accomplish our goals? What is the timeline for each step?
Support Needed	What types of support do we need to accomplish each step? What material resources are necessary?
Forward	After a stage of implementation, take time to reflect, refine your plan, and move forward with next steps.

Tool 53B Template for PRESS Forward

PRESS Forward	
Purpose	
Relationships and Connections	
Expected Outcomes	
Steps to Take	
Support Needed	
Forward	

Final Thoughts and Action Planning

The most effective schools are those that are committed to the continual professional growth and development of all personnel. They recognize the importance of investing in people and assuring that they have the knowledge and skills needed for continued success. Professional learning communities and other collaborative structures provide a mechanism for teachers, principals, and other staff to make the improvement of student learning a priority.

One of the most valuable tools you can use to achieve your vision of a more rigorous school is a focused, standards-based, high quality professional development program. Reflect using the Action Plan.

My Action Plan for Professional Development

The most important tool from this chapter in my current situation is:

_____

_____

_____

_____

I also think the following concepts and/or tools would be useful in my situation:

_____

_____

_____

_____

I need additional help or resources in the form of:

_____

_____

_____

_____

My next action steps are to:

_____

_____

_____

_____

7

Advocacy

Whether you recognize it or not, you are an advocate, always advocating for your school and the resources and programs to improve the educational experience of your students. It is one of your important roles.

Advocacy is what you do when you are actively supporting a cause like increasing the rigor of your school. It is often compared to public relations. But advocacy is quite different. When a leader advocates for their program they are committed to providing information to stakeholder groups that will build support for their vision of increased rigor. They recognize the importance of building networks and alliances that will support their efforts

Advocacy is a way to effectively press for change. It is also the foundation of our democracy and a process that allows ordinary people to shape and influence policy at all levels. Identifying priorities, crafting a strategy, taking action, and achieving results are critical steps to finding one's voice, making oneself heard, and shaping one's future.

Tools in Chapter Seven: Advocacy	
Tool 54	Self-Assess Your Advocacy Skills
Tool 55	Seven Step Planning Process
Tool 56	Designing An Advocacy Plan
Tool 57	Stakeholders in Your School
Tool 58	Working with Internal Stakeholders
Tool 59	Movers and Shakers
Tool 60	Build a Network
Tool 61	The One Page Fact Sheet
Tool 62	Elevator Talk
Tool 63	Parent and Family Advocacy Tools
Tool 64	Advocacy with Your School Board
Tool 65	Dealing with the Media
Tool 66	Assessment of Technology
Tool 67	Advocacy Scorecard

Tool 54 – Self-Assess Your Advocacy Skills

You may be unsure about your advocacy skills. Throughout this chapter, we'll provide specific tools that can help you. However, there are some key characteristics that are also important. Tool 54-Self-Assess Your Advocacy Skills will guide your reflections.

TOOL 54   Self-Assess Your Advocacy Skills

	I already do this	I need to work on this
Speak from the heart when telling their story.		
Speak to the local impact and implications.		
Be factual and honest. Be clear, concise, and concrete.		
Develop sound bites, success stories, elevator talks, and one page fact sheets.		

	I already do this	I need to work on this
Frame the issue and tie it to a larger picture.		
Be cheerfully persistent. Know their audience and build their advocacy appropriately.		
Don't forget to follow up and say thank you.		

What are your current strengths that you can build upon?

_____

_____

_____

_____

What are your top three areas for improvement?

_____

_____

_____

_____

Tool 55 – Seven Step Planning Process

In Tool 55-Seven Step Planning Process, we've identified a seven-step process that can help you develop a plan to build support for your efforts to increase the rigor of your school.

Tool 55 Seven Step Planning Process

1. Analyze your environment: Scan the environment in which your school exists: district, community, state, nation, and word. Identify the issues that affect your school and those that affect your community more broadly.

2. Monitor changes in your environment: Read voraciously, talk with a wide selection of people in your community (see Tool 59-Movers and Shakers), and stay current with trends at the state and national level.

3. Identify the factors needed for success: Look beyond traditional factors (good teachers, money) and consider emerging issues such as the acquisition and use of technology or the ability to respond to changing conditions. Consider groups in your community with which you can partner.

4. Think about your assumptions: Identify the assumptions you hold about your school and its environment. Test them by assessing the degree of certainty (high, medium, low) and the level of impact (high, medium, low). Assumptions play an important role in constructing the future.

5. Develop a vision of an alternative future: Consider the issue of rigor at your school and identify the factors you identified as critical for success. Develop a vision of the future that is different from current circumstances. Creating several alternatives is better.

6. Consider allies and opponents: Identify individuals or groups that may support your efforts as well as those who may resist. Be sure and include those you know and those that may emerge. Develop a plan for building alliances with your allies and bridges to enlighten your opposition.

7. Develop a plan for advocating for your desired future: Identify specific steps that can be taken to achieve the anticipated future. Develop both "hedging strategies" that can cope with undesirable futures and "shaping strategies" that help create the desired future.

8. Remember, education is an issue that crosses political party lines. A nonpartisan focus will help you as an advocate.

Adapted from: Marx (2006) and Williamson and Blackburn (2009)

Tool 56 – Designing An Advocacy Plan

Crafting an advocacy plan includes several distinct steps. Tool 56-Designing An Advocacy Plan summarizes the steps. First and foremost is to be clear about the issue. Be as specific as you can about what you want to achieve. For example, your focus may be increasing the rigor of instruction in classrooms at your school.

Then you need to identify goals and accompanying strategies, learn about your allies and opponents and those who might emerge as allies or opponents, and develop advocacy strategies and identify opportunities to impact their thinking. Finally, you need to implement your plan and monitor its results.

Tool 56 Designing An Advocacy Plan

Step 1: Identify the issue.

Step 2: Be clear about your goals and accompanying strategies.

Step 3: Identify strengths and weaknesses of your current status.

Step 4: Develop specific strategies and identify advocacy opportunities.

Step 5: Implement strategies.

Step 6: Monitor plan and assess results.

Step 7: Adjust plan as needed.

A more detailed discussion about planning, implementing, and sustaining a plan to achieve your vision for a more rigorous school is included in Chapter Two.

What if...

"I don't understand. We've already developed a plan for increasing rigor. How is this different or does it fit within that plan?"

Your advocacy plan shapes your communication with people in your school community: teachers, families, district staff and school board, and community members. An advocacy plan is designed to build support for your vision and share your success.

Be Clear About Stakeholders

Every school community has both internal and external stakeholders, people who have a 'stake' in the success of your school. It's easy to focus on the groups inside your school, but groups outside the school also have a 'stake' in your success. They often shape public opinion and influence decision-makers.

Examples of Stakeholder Groups	
Internal	External
♦ teachers	♦ families
♦ other staff	♦ school board
♦ students	♦ business leaders
♦ administrative team	♦ senior citizens
	♦ neighbors without children in the school
	♦ media

Now, use Tool 57-Stakeholders in Your School to think about your own school community and identify the specific stakeholder groups.

Tool 57   Stakeholders in Your School

Stakeholder Groups	
Internal	External

Each group will have differing needs for information and you may need to develop a diverse set of strategies to inform them of your work and engage them as partners in your work to improve the rigor of your school.

Internal Stakeholders

In Chapter Four, we talked about ways to involve and inform stakeholders, including internal groups. First, it is important to recognize that everyone who works or attends your school may not have the same level of support for increasing rigor. Second, regardless of their support, you must develop a plan to work with staff members to nurture and sustain momentum toward your vision. Use Tool 58-Working with Internal Stakeholders to consider your own situation.

What if...

"Who are my internal stakeholders? Do you mean my teachers, or more than that?"

We will address external stakeholders on page 130, and that may help clarify the difference between internal and external stakeholders. Internal stakeholders are those people you would consider "school insiders," those who are actively working in your school. This certainly includes your faculty and staff, but it also would include those volunteers who are regularly in your building. We would also consider parents, family members, or community members who serve on your School Improvement Council or other active committees to be internal stakeholders. Don't get caught up in the labels; focus on using the strategies to work with those involved in the school.

TOOL 58 Working with Internal Stakeholders

	How do I already do this?	How do I need to create other opportunities for this?
Create opportunities for teachers and other staff to be involved in planning to increase rigor.		
Provide multiple forms of professional development to help increase capacity for improving rigor.		
Communicate in a variety of ways.		
Engage both supporters and detractors in conversations about rigor and strategies for improving rigor in your school.		
Attend to your own professional growth and development about rigor.		
Model the use of rigor in your daily interactions with staff.		
Share examples of best practices from within your school and from other sites.		
Understand that not everyone will embrace your vision.		

External Stakeholders

Schools do not exist in isolation. They are part of the fabric of every community and reflect community values and priorities. The external community, like your internal community, is comprised of groups with very different needs for information and access to the school. Examples of external stakeholders include families, the school board, business community, senior citizens, neighbors of the school, and the media.

Tool 59 – Movers and Shakers

Every community has a set of "movers and shakers." They are individuals who are recognized leaders in their area, ones who others turn to for guidance on important issues. Each is someone who is able to get things done by rallying support, identifying resources, and building coalitions.

Characteristics of "Movers and Shakers"

- ◆ articulate spokesperson
- ◆ respected for their knowledge
- ◆ ability to convince others of their point-of-view
- ◆ skilled at identifying and securing resources
- ◆ connected to other "movers and shakers"
- ◆ wield power and influence
- ◆ often energetic and initiate change
- ◆ seen as able to influence the future

Think about your own school. Who would you identify on Tool 59-Movers and Shakers? You may list a parent, but there might also be a "mover and shaker" who does not have children in your school. Also describe why you included each person on your list. Move throughout the tool to consider your school district. Who are the "movers and shakers" in your district? What characteristics do they possess? Finally, consider people outside your immediate area. Frequently, the most influential "movers and shakers" are outside of your school or district. They may be influential politicians, policy makers, or community development personnel.

Tool 59 Movers and Shakers

Movers and Shakers in Your School	
Names 1. 2. 3. 4. 5.	Characteristics 1. 2. 3. 4. 5.

Movers and Shakers in Your District	
Names 1. 2. 3. 4. 5.	Characteristics 1. 2. 3. 4. 5.

Movers and Shakers Beyond Your School and District	
Names 1. 2. 3. 4. 5.	Characteristics 1. 2. 3. 4. 5.

What if...

"I'm struggling with my list. Some of the people who are movers and shakers aren't supporters of the school. Do I still need to consider them?"

Yes. A mover and shaker is someone who is influential and has the ability to convince others of their point-of-view. Since they are respected for their knowledge on a topic, it is important to develop a plan for sharing information with them that might change their opinion.

One district where we worked sought "known dissenters" to be involved in improvement projects. After all, you'll hear from them sooner than later. So, the district brought them into the process early. Imagine the impact when a known dissenter is part of a group supporting one of your initiatives.

There's no assurance that providing information or involving them in improvement projects will change their minds. But it certainly can't hurt.

Advocacy Tools

Successful advocacy is more than just passion for your vision of a more rigorous school. It requires that you develop a set of strategies to share your message and mobilize others to support your vision.

Tool 60 – Build a Network

To be truly effective, you need to build a network of people who can help with your efforts. Remember, communication is a two-way street, so this group will serve two purposes: to help you understand how stakeholders in various groups perceive a situation and to help you communicate your message.

One model is the Key Communicator Network, developed by the National School Public Relations Association. It includes a series of steps that help you identify key people to invite to participate and ideas for how you can work with them to advocate for your vision.

Tool 60A   Building A Key Communicator Network

1. Bring together a small group of trusted people who know the community. Brainstorm with those whom others listen to. While the bank president may be an opinion leader, so might the barber, cab driver, bartender, or supermarket checkout clerk.

2. Create a workable list from all the names that have been gathered to invite to join your network. Make sure that all segments of the community are represented.

3. Send a letter to the potential members, explaining that you want to create a new communications group for your school to help the community understand the challenges, successes, and activities of your school. In the letter, invite the potential members to an initial meeting and include a response form.

4. Make follow-up phone calls to those who do not return the response form, especially those who will be most important to have on your network.

5. Start the initial meeting by explaining that those in the audience have been invited because you see them as respected community members who care about the education students are being provided. Also, point out that you believe schools operate best when the community understands what is taking place and becomes involved in providing the best possible learning opportunities for students. Then, describe the objectives of a Key Communicator Network:

   ♦ to provide network members with honest, objective, consistent information about the school

   ♦ to have the network members deliver this information to others in the community when they are asked questions or in other opportunities, and

   ♦ to keep their ears open for any questions or concerns community members might have about the school. Those concerns should be reported to the principal or person in charge of the network so communication efforts can deal with those concerns. (It's always best to learn about concerns when one or two people have them instead of when 20 or 30 are vocally sharing them with others.)

   Ask the invitees for a commitment to serve on the network and find out the best way to communicate with them, i.e. email, fax, or telephone.

6. Establish a Key Communicator Network newsletter specifically for these people. After the first year, send out a short evaluation form to see how the network is working and might be improved.

> For more information about Key Communicator Networks, contact the National School Public Relations Association, 301.519.0496 and purchase a copy of *A Guidebook for Opinion Leader/Key Communicator Programs.*

Now think about your own school community. How would you build a Key Communicator Network? Use Tool 60B-Creating Your Key Communicator Network to plan your strategies.

Tool 60B   Creating Your Key Communicator Network

1. Who would you bring together to talk about building a network? Who would you talk with about the group? How would you assure all segments of your community are represented?	
2. How will you extend an invitation to potential members and explain the purpose of the group? How will you create a sense of urgency and importance for their participation?	
3. How do you plan to organize the initial meeting? Where will the meeting be held? How will you share your vision? How will you listen and gather feedback from members?	
4. What process will you use to both gather and share information with the network? How ill you keep members engaged in the work?	

Tool 61 – The One Page Fact Sheet

A "One Page Fact Sheet" helps you organize the important facts and points of your issue. It can be used as a handout to be shared with others and it will give you necessary background information, as well as added confidence to discuss your issue. One page is your limit. Most decision makers want the basic facts and don't want wasted time. The limit also enables you to keep your message focused.

Tool 61A   Key Points in a One Page Fact Sheet

Clearly define the issue

State your position on the issue.

Clarify what you want the decision maker to do.

Define five talking points in order of importance.

Provide two references to support issue.

Make the sale with a closure statement.

Mike Matkovich, a teacher-leader, used this process to develop a one-page fact sheet related to increasing rigor at his high school. With his permission, we adapted it slightly for illustrative purposes. After you review his sample, use Tool 61C-Your One Page Fact Sheet to write your own.

Tool 61B Sample One Page Fact Sheet: Increasing Rigor at XXX High School

Our Goal: To provide students with high quality and high intensity classes in high school for post-secondary success.

Recommendation: Implement a thorough review of all courses and support appropriate revisions to ensure that each of our students is prepared for post-secondary success.

Important Facts:

- Most Americans do not believe that schools provide a rigorous enough high school experience.
- The fastest growing part of the high school curriculum at the moment is AP classes or college level courses. The fastest growing part of the college curriculum is remedial or high school classes.
- Student readiness for college-level reading is at its lowest point in more than a decade. Additionally, high school tests address content that does not exceed the 9th or 10th grade.
- The most common misconception about college readiness is that meeting their high school graduation requirements prepares them for college. High schools in states with more demanding graduation standards make more progress in advancing student achievement than schools in states with less rigorous standards.
- Improving college readiness is crucial to the development of a diverse and talented labor force that is able to maintain and increase U.S. economic competitiveness throughout the world.

Our Situation:

Less than 30% of our students take advanced courses. Even though 95% of our students pass the exit exam, they are not necessarily prepared for college. 15% of our students lose their scholarships at the end of their freshman year, due to a low GPA. A recent outside evaluation recommended that we increase rigor in all classes.

References:

www.act.org   www.sreb.org

TOOL 61C   Your One Page Fact Sheet

The Issue: _____

_____

_____

_____

Your Position on the Issue: _____

_____

_____

_____

_____

_____

_____

What You Want Person to Do: _____

_____

_____

_____

_____

_____

_____

Talking Points (include compelling data): _____

_____

_____

_____

_____

_____

References: _____

_____

_____

_____

_____

_____

Tool 62 – Elevator Talk

There are times when you only have a brief opportunity to make personal contact with a key decision maker. As the old adage says, you only have one chance to make a first impression. In those cases, you should be prepared to give a personal story about the importance of your issue: increasing rigor. Elevator talks should only be for a one- or two-story building—the time it takes an elevator to travel one or two floors—and no more than 30 seconds. People tire quickly of tedious talk about an issue, particularly when part of a casual encounter.

Tool 62A   Elements of An Elevator Talk

1. Your name and what you do

2. Your key issue

3. What you would like the person to know

Practice telling your story and why you care about this issue with another person. This will give you confidence when you have a chance or planned meeting with a stakeholder or "mover and shaker." Having an effective "elevator talk" is essential in networking, engaging partners, and opening new doors. First impressions are easily sabotaged with an elevator talk that's unimpressive because it's too long or too short.

Use the three characteristics to develop a draft of your talk using Tool 62B-Elevator Talk Plan.

Tool 62B   Elevator Talk Plan

Your name and what you do: _____

_____

Your key issue: _____

_____

_____

_____

What you would like the person to know: _____

_____

_____

_____

_____

_____

_____

Next, refine your talk. Read your notes, then reflect using Tool 62C-Try This.

Tool 62C   Try This

Imagine you want to explain to fifth graders the importance of greater rigor in classrooms. Use no jargon or fuzzy words, just simple talk. Now increase the grade level while maintaining the simplicity. Use 20 words or less. Refine and edit your presentation until you have a creative way of conveying your message that stimulates the listener to support your effort.

Finally, write your polished message using Tool 62D-Final Elevator Talk. Refer to it often, and use it when needed.

Tool 62D   Final Elevator Talk

_____

_____

_____

_____

_____

_____

_____

_____

_____

_____

_____

_____

_____

_____

_____

_____

_____

_____

_____

_____

_____

_____

Advocacy with Parents and Families

Parents and families are important allies in improving your school's program. Not only do they support your efforts with their children, they can be advocates for your school with their friends, extended family, and connections throughout the community.

There are three strategies for your advocacy work with families. First, communicate often and with lots of information. Second, provide meaningful roles for parents in school life so that they can see your work to improve rigor. Third, provide support and resources so that they can be successful with their children at home. Using Tool 63-Parent and Family Advocacy Tools, consider the three strategies, your current efforts in that area, and other options you might implement.

TOOL 63 Parent and Family Advocacy Tools

Strategy	How We Do This Now	What We Need to Consider
Communication Strategies (include a variety of media including print and electronic)		
Provide Meaningful Involvement (provide ways for families to be involved beyond traditional PTO and bake sales)		
Provide Support and Resources (identify information and resources needed to work with their children)		

What if...

"My biggest challenge as we try to increase rigor is our parents. They say they want higher levels of rigor, but when our teachers have high standards and grade appropriately, then many parents are upset that their children aren't making straight A's."

We talk with lots of parents when we visit schools and we've found that the concern about grades almost always masks a deeper concern that their children will not be able to achieve the higher standards. Our three-part definition of rigor includes high support and rigorous assessment that includes things like opportunities for students to revise and resubmit. The focus on rigor is all about improving student learning. You need to provide parents with a specific plan for supporting students when you talk about increasing rigor.

Tool 64 – Advocacy with Your School Board

Your school board sets district policies and determines the allocation of funds. Board members are often community leaders who have influence with other members of the community. By gathering support from the school board you can build momentum for your plans through the networks and alliance of board members.

Your school board is different from any other stakeholder group. Because they set policy and allocate resources, it is important to always connect your vision of increasing rigor with the board's vision for the district.

There are some other steps that we've found to be really important when interacting with your school board. After reviewing the suggestions, you can use Tool 64B-Your Plan for Talking with Your School Board to draft your own plan.

TOOL 64A   Strategies for Interacting with Your School Board

♦ Identify a parent or community spokesperson to help deliver your message to the board.

♦ Frame the importance of rigor in your opening statement. Link it to board goals and how students will be successful once they leave your school.

♦ Describe your plan in such a way that the board can see the link between your overall school improvement efforts and their goals.

♦ Share examples of your work to illustrate the impact. It can be very helpful to highlight the effect of greater rigor on one or more students.

♦ Give recognition to the individuals who have contributed to your success. It is a time for you to be modest and allow others to be recognized.

♦ Conclude your presentation by aligning your vision of improved rigor with the board's vision for the district.

TOOL 64B Your Plan for Talking with Your School Board

What parent or community spokesperson might be helpful in talking with the Board?

_____

_____

_____

_____

_____

_____

How would we describe the importance of rigor and our plans for improving rigor?

_____

_____

_____

_____

_____

_____

How will we discuss our plan, our successes, and the impact on students?

_____

_____

_____

_____

_____

How will you connect your current plans with your vision of a more rigorous school and with the board's vision for the district?

_____

_____

_____

_____

_____

_____

_____

What if...

"Is talking with my school board that different? Shouldn't I just say the same things I tell everyone else?"

No, the school board is different. They set policy for the district and allocate resources. Their responsibility is the welfare of the entire district. Because most boards have a vision for their district, it is vitally important to link your vision with theirs so that they can see how your efforts support their goals.

Advocacy and the Media

At some point, you will likely be required to deal with the media, whether it is your local newspaper or some form of electronic media. Don't be taken by surprise; anticipate that you will need to communicate with the media and plan appropriately. Preparation is your friend. You might keep Tool 65-Dealing with the Media immediately available as a reminder of ways you can be an effective advocate with the media.

TOOL 65   Dealing with the Media

- Preparation is your best friend. Learn as much as you can about the reporter, the show, and the audience.
- Establish your communication goals for each interview.
- Determine two or three key points to make to reach your goal.
- Speak in "memorable language."
- Learn and use the "bridging technique." Redirect the interview to your key points.
- Practice, practice, practice. Practice on camera if possible.
- Do not wear clothes or use mannerisms that distract from your message.
- Forget jargon, now and forever.
- Make sure that the mind is in gear before the mouth travels.
- Look at the reporter when answering questions; turn to the camera when delivering a key point.
- Steady eyes suggest honesty; blinking, darting eyes suggest nervousness and dishonesty.
- Anticipate questions and have answers ready. Once the interview is scheduled, try to figure out what questions the reporter might ask.
- Relax.

Advocacy and Emerging Technology

Traditional media should be part of an advocacy plan but emerging technology can also be helpful to your efforts. You may want to use Tool 66-Assessment of Technology to consider ways that "new" technology, including social media, can help mobilize your community to support your school program. For example, examine your school's website to see if it communicates your vision. Does it showcase ways that parents can be involved? Use social media like Twitter, Facebook, and other sites to share information with parents about your school, its program, and successes.

TOOL 66   Assessment of Technology

	Strengths	Opportunities
School Website ♦ Does your school have a website? If so, how frequently is information updated? ♦ Does it include your vision of a more rigorous school? ♦ Does it provide information families can use to work with their children? ♦ Does it provide ways families can become involved in your school?		
Social Media Sites ♦ Does your school have a presence on social networking sites (Twitter, Facebook)? ♦ If so, how do you share information about school events and successes? ♦ Do parents know your school has a presence on these sites?		

Tool 67 – Advocacy Scorecard

Barbara's father is a successful advocate in North Carolina where he provides information about the importance of healthy lifestyles for children and adolescents. He shared with us a strategy for assessing the status of your advocacy efforts. We've adapted his work into Tool 67-Advocacy Scorecard, which principals can use to measure their advocacy work.

TOOL 67 Advocacy Scorecard

Directions: Score your advocacy work by awarding 1–10 points for each of the following items.

_____ 1. My school has a written plan to partner with others.

_____ 2. We are open to building partnerships with other schools and groups.

_____ 3. We build links to websites as a way to assist our partners.

_____ 4. We know how to communicate effectively with other groups.

_____ 5. We understand the human relations skills necessary for our partners to work successfully together.

_____ 6. We understand the cultures that every school and organization brings to our partnership work.

_____ 7. We enjoy sharing successes with our partners.

_____ 8. There is regular, routine communication among our local, district, and state partners.

_____ 9. We understand the pitfalls of working with partners and have developed strategies for avoiding them.

_____ 10. We partner with other schools and with agencies in education and related fields in support of our vision for greater rigor.

0–20	Do you really want to be an advocate?
21–40	It's time to think about what you do.
41–60	You have a solid foundation for advocacy.
61–80	You know the meaning of empowerment.
81–100	You have an excellent plan for advocacy.

How did you do? Where are your strengths as an advocate and where are opportunities for growth?

Final Thoughts and Action Planning

As a school leader, you find yourself advocating for your school. You talk with teachers and other staff. You talk with families. You build networks with community groups inside and outside of education and you interact with people in the central office. It is important for leaders to recognize this important role and strengthen their skills to hone a clear message about the importance of increasing rigor in schools. Use the Action Plan to describe your plans.

My Action Plan for Advocacy

The most important tool from this chapter in my current situation is:

_____

_____

_____

_____

_____

I also think the following concepts and/or tools would be useful in my situation:

_____

_____

_____

_____

_____

I need additional help or resources in the form of:

_____

_____

_____

_____

_____

My next action steps are to:

_____

_____

_____

_____

_____

8

Shared Accountability

Despite the different levels of acceptance of any change effort, it will not be successful unless there is shared accountability for its implementation and its success. Our beliefs about accountability are clear. We believe that accountability resides in every stakeholder group: teachers, administrators, students, families, and community, as well as district leadership.

Accountability is much more than issuing mandates and holding people accountable. The most successful school leaders understand that it involves energizing and motivating individuals and groups.

Shared accountability does not just happen. It must be an integral part of your planning at every stage. In Chapter Three: Culture and Chapter Four: Ownership and Shared Vision, we described a variety of strategies that are helpful to engage all stakeholders in building a rigorous learning environment. Discussions of shared accountability as a part of those processes will be foundational to your success.

Tools in Chapter Eight: Shared Accountability	
Tool 68	Assess Your Work in This Area
Tool 69	Walkthroughs
Tool 70	Classroom Observations
Tool 71	Accountability through Professional Development
Tool 72	Analysis of School Improvement Plan
Tool 73	Accountability For Families and Community
Tool 74	Homework Help Tips for Parents
Tool 75	Ways to Support Student Accountability
Tool 76	Rigor through Requiring Demonstration of Learning

Progress occurs where there is a collective commitment to improvement and a parallel commitment to supporting people who take risks and make changes. First and foremost, teachers and principals must focus on improving the instructional experience of every student. Every student must be expected to learn and the staff must be committed to supporting students in their learning. Failure cannot be an option. School personnel must work with families and community members to assure that students have the resources to be successful in school, and families must be engaged in school life through participation in school governance and responsibility for student success.

The most important role for a school leader is supervisor of the instructional program. But we recognize that leaders are not the only ones responsible for a quality instructional program. Teachers and other staff are responsible for delivering instruction and positively impacting every student's learning.

Accountability for Your Own Actions

Leaders, however, have a significant role in creating a climate and culture that supports rigorous, quality instruction; promotes innovation; and nurtures professional growth. As the old adage notes, "If you're going to talk the talk, you've got to walk the walk." Before we discuss accountability from others, take time to self-reflect. Tool 68-Assess Your Work in This Area will provide guidance for this process.

TOOL 68   Assess Your Work in This Area

Do these statements describe you as a leader? Use the following scale: 1 – Strongly Disagree 3–Neutral 5 – Strongly Agree 2 – Disagree 4 – Agree	Rating
I create a structure that provides time for collegial discussion and dialogue about increasing rigor.	
I stay current on educational trends and developments.	
I access professional development and other resources to support more rigorous classrooms.	
I model rigorous instructional practices at meetings and during other interactions with staff.	
I am attentive to my own professional development and attend and actively participate in professional development and other learning opportunities about improving rigor.	
I talk with teachers about their work to improve rigor in their classrooms.	
I routinely visit classrooms specifically to observe and learn about our work to improve rigor.	
I talk with families and community about our efforts to improve rigor in our school.	
Areas for Improvement:	

What if...

"How can I find time for this in addition to everything else I'm doing? Even if I want to do this, other things seem to get in my way."

One of the biggest challenges for school leaders is juggling multiple priorities. Ultimately, what the leader pays attention to becomes important. So it is important to develop a system for prioritizing your tasks and managing your time. One principal we met in Michigan worked with her administrative assistant to schedule one hour a day for classroom visits. It became a scheduled appointment and when people called and wanted to see the principal they were told she was in a meeting (which she was). A friend of ours, Frank Buck, has really good ideas about time management. His blog (http://frankbuck.blogspot.com) offers lots of useful tips for principals.

Accountability for Faculty and Staff

While the most important role of a school leader is to supervise the instructional program, he or she is not the only person responsible. Every employee of the school shares in the accountability. By participating in professional development, working to improve their performance, and working collaboratively with colleagues, they contribute to the shared accountability present in effective schools.

Accountability through Supervisory Practices

Effective supervision is an ongoing process, not a one-time event. It is much more than just evaluating teacher performance. It is all about engaging teachers in reflective conversations about their practice.

Effective supervisors understand that teachers are adults and respond well to the principles of adult learning. Effective supervisors are empowering and motivating and recognize the importance of providing time for teachers to reflect on and think about their teaching.

Tool 69 – Walkthroughs

One concept that has grown in popularity is the "walkthrough." Depending on the model you follow, this can range from a structured approach to simply dropping in for a few minutes. Walkthroughs can be effective to gain a general sense of what is going on in classrooms as opposed to evaluating individual teachers.

We've developed a walkthrough protocol that can be used to measure progress on increasing rigor. A portion of the protocol is provided in Tool 69A-Criteria for Evidence: Rigorous Schools and Classrooms.

Tool 69A Criteria for Evidence: Rigorous Schools and Classrooms

Elements and Indicators	Observations and Questions
Learner-Centered Instruction ♦ Teachers maintain high expectations for all students. ♦ Support and scaffolding are provided to ensure success. ♦ There is evidence of high order student thinking. ♦ Students are active in all aspects of learning. ♦ Lessons seamlessly incorporate application activities.	
Expectations for Learning ♦ Teachers are consistent in the belief that students can learn, will learn, and that they have the power to help them do so. ♦ Lessons are designed so students see the value of specific learning. ♦ Teachers are persistent in supporting student learning. ♦ Interaction with students reflects the belief that it is unacceptable not to learn.	
Support for Student Learning ♦ Teachers work to remove barriers to student success. ♦ A repertoire of strategies is used to interact with students. ♦ Teachers use positive strategies to encourage student learning. ♦ Students receive high quality feedback about their work.	
Demonstrating Student Learning ♦ Each student regularly demonstrates his or her understanding of content. ♦ Multiple ways to demonstrate learning are included in lessons.	
School as Learning Community ♦ Every member of the school believes that it is unacceptable not to learn. ♦ Teachers meet and plan together to support student learning. ♦ Teachers use multiple types of data to make decisions about student learning. ♦ Teachers work and learn together.	
Date: Observer:	

In Tool 69B-Pasadena ISD Walkthrough Form, you'll see an adapted alternate form used by Pasadena Independent School District in Texas. Originally, they evaluated quadrants related to Rigor and Relevance (Daggett, 2010), which works within our model. However, we adapted it to incorporate our broader view of looking for the teacher's connection to students' values as a motivational strategy and to include our definition.

Tool 69B   Pasadena ISD Walkthrough Form

Pasadena ISD Walkthrough Form (Adapted, Blackburn and Williamson)

Teacher Name Observer Name

Subject Start/end Time Date

✓ Indicates positive use of **X** Indicates a concern **?** Indicates a question

Domain I: Active, Successful Student Participation

Student Engagement
_Active Participation Student Dialogue Compliance
_Student Engagement Level 90% 89-80% 79-70% <70%

Student Successful in Learning
_Works independently Participates in group work Responds to question(s)
_Initiates or completes work with apparent ease

Learning Made Relevant
_Relevant Examples Real World Materials/Resources Relevant Task(s) Assigned

Grouping
_Independent Partners Small Group Whole Group

*Do all students demonstrate learning (rigor)?*_____
_____
_____

Domain II: Learner Centered

Is each student held to high expectations (rigor)? _____
_____
_____

Instructional Strategies
_Vocabulary Summarizing Student Dialogue
_Metaphor, Simile, Analogy Writing to Learn Cooperative Grouping
_Graphic Organizer Notetaking Lab Work
_Charts, Graphs, Maps, Tables Scaffolded Questioning Manipulatives
_5 E Model Differentiated Materials

Learning Objectives
_Content Objective(s) posted using Student Expectation language
_Learning Objective(s) posted in terms of Listening Speaking Reading Writing
_Objectives aligned to TEKS and PISD Scope and Sequence
_Objectives used in instruction; checks for understanding or for informal assessments
_SE/Learning Objectives are congruent to assigned student tasks
_Instruction, materials, and strategies congruent with posted SE

Value/Motivation
_Is value of lesson evident to learner? Evidence:

Release of the Learning to the Learner
_Explain and Describe Shared Guided Independent

Embedded Technology
_Utilization of multi-media and visuals
_Utilization of Interactive Board by teacher student(s)
_Utilization of projector
_Utilization of calculators
_Utilization of Active Student Response System(s)
_Integration of Internet resources

Domain III: Evaluation and Feedback on Student Progress

Questioning for Formal or Informal Assessment
_Volunteer Responses Non-Volunteer Responses Global Open-ended
_Utilization of "wait time" Use of student response to adjust instruction

Feedback and Active Monitoring
_Teacher Circulating/Scanning Whole group or small group Re-direction
_Individual Re-direction Reteach/Clarify
_Response(s) address students' thinking/questions
_Student work posted Not observed

Are all students supported for learning (rigor)? _____
_____
_____

If Testing
_Multiple Choice Open-ended Combination of MC/Open
_Teacher monitoring Students testing without teacher assistance/clarification
_Congruent with TAKS/EOC /AP/SAT Rigorous

_____
_____
_____

Domain IV: Management of Student Discipline, Instructional Strategies, Time

Students Demonstrates Established Classroom Routines and Procedures
_Routines clearly established Positive learning environment
_Positive rapport w/students Appropriate use of humor
_Specific and positive reinforcement (3:1 Ratio) Student compliance to posted expectations
_Excellent classroom management techniques used

Effective and Efficient Use of Instructional Time
_Warm-up Smooth transitions Lesson closure by teacher
_Lesson closed with appropriate student activity
_Utilizes entire instructional period for learning
_Instructional materials and resources are prepared in advance
_Instructional materials and resources are systematically managed

Redirects Disruptive or Disengaged Behavior
_Respectful redirect/re-engagement with no disruption of lesson
_De-escalates inappropriate behavior with minimal disruption of lesson/class
_Teacher provides for movement and/or grouping changes as needed
_Classroom exclusion is appropriately handled by teacher
_"Just in Time" student conference/redirect methods used by teacher
_Evidence of CHAMPS training Evidence of Conscious Discipline training

General Comments _____

_____
_____
_____

Teacher Signature Date

Observer Signature Date

What if...

"We've tried walkthroughs in the past, but my teachers feel like I can't get a true picture of their teaching in such a short time. How should I respond?"

You can't. A walkthrough is just a snapshot, not a complete movie. Talk about this with your teachers and let them know that you recognize the limits of a walkthrough. We've found that the most effective use of walkthroughs is when teachers and administrators work together to identify the focus and to conduct the walkthroughs. Always disconnect the walkthrough from evaluation. Not every good teaching practice is used in every lesson, nor will they always be visible when you visit a classroom.

Tool 70 – Classroom Observations

Every school district has an established evaluation process including established timelines and forms. We recognize the legal requirements that principals must meet. But we also believe it is important for principals to visit classrooms and observe teaching throughout the year.

Formative feedback to a teacher is often more helpful than a summative evaluation. It provides an opportunity for the teachers to reflect on their work and continue to strengthen and refine their teaching practices.

We especially like a model that includes an opportunity for a pre-conference with the teacher where you talk about the students, the design of the lesson, and any other relevant information. Following the observation, a post-observation conference provides an opportunity to talk with the teacher about the lesson.

We've developed an observation protocol that reflects our three-part definition of rigor. It reflects our belief that such tools are best when you can provide the teacher with specific feedback about their work. Therefore, we included a place for you to describe the evidence you saw about each teacher action.

Tool 70A-Classroom Observation Protocol provides an observation form we use. Central to using this protocol is the recognition that every characteristic of a rigorous classroom will not be present in each lesson. We believe it is important to look for patterns that develop over multiple classroom visits.

TOOL 70A Classroom Observation Protocol

Teacher: _____ Date: _____

Grade/Subject: _____

Instructions: Rate each item on a scale from 1 to 5 with 1 indicating low implementation and 5 indicating high implementation. Provide evidence gathered during the classroom observation to support the rating.

The teacher...	Rating and Evidence Observed
1. Acts consistently on the unwavering belief that each student can and will learn, and on the teacher's power to help them do so.	Rating: Evidence:
2. Regularly provides support and scaffolding needed to ensure each student's success.	Rating: Evidence:
3. Provides support that is customized so that students are not allowed not to learn.	Rating: Evidence:
4. Allows each student to demonstrate his or her understanding of content in ways that are appropriately challenging.	Rating: Evidence:
5. Makes sure that all students are actively engaged in learning by making connections and contributing to the discussion.	Rating: Evidence:
6. Builds appropriate support into every lesson.	Rating: Evidence:

continued

Tool 70A   Classroom Observation Protocol (*continued*)

The teacher...	Rating and Evidence Observed
7. Uses questions that are uniformly high quality and provide opportunity for students to extend their learning.	Rating: Evidence:
8. Provides consistently high quality feedback that students can use to improve their work.	Rating: Evidence:
9. Uses a broad repertoire of strategies to interact with students about instruction and student learning.	Rating: Evidence:
10. Uses verbal and nonverbal cues to let students know that they can be successful.	Rating: Evidence:
11. Includes adequate time for students to respond throughout each lesson.	Rating: Evidence:
12. Designs lessons so that the majority of activities are interactive, and whole group activities are limited.	Rating: Evidence:

We think the best data is collected over multiple observations, rather than relying on a single observation. We also believe that the most productive conversations about rigor occur following the classroom observation. Teachers value the time to think about their work and reflect on its success.

Reflection is a critical part of implementing any instructional innovation. Often the most skilled teachers are most interested in an opportunity to reflect on their teaching and consider ways to grow professionally.

Open-ended questions tend to be better than one-word, closed-ended questions. They do not lend themselves to a single answer and are designed to promote teacher reflection. The discussion cannot be seen as evaluative, nor punitive. It must be supportive and encourage professional growth. Tool 70B-Post-Observation Discussion Prompts can guide your planning.

TOOL 70B Post-Observation Discussion Prompts

Examples of Post-Observation Discussion Prompts	Other Discussion Prompts I Would Like to Use
◆ Thank you for the opportunity to visit your classroom. I would like to have you talk with me about the lesson. ◆ When you plan a lesson, what things do you consider? How do you plan to address our goal of improved rigor for students? ◆ Describe ways that you monitor student learning during your lessons? What clues do you gather about student learning? ◆ How do you consider the value of the lesson for the students? Do they see the relevance of learning? ◆ As you continue to implement _____, what do you consider the appropriate next steps? ◆ What additional support or resources may I provide for you? How can I support your effort to improve the rigor in your classroom?	

Tool 71 – Accountability through Professional Development

Professional development is an essential tool for achieving your vision of a more rigorous school. In Chapter Seven, we shared some common approaches like book studies and looking at student work, as well as some different approaches like lesson study and using a charrette.

Beyond providing professional development, it is also critical that you assure accountability for the use of professional development. At one school where Ron worked, teachers were responsible for sharing one new idea they implemented at the first staff meeting after any professional development activity. They met in small groups, shared their ideas, and asked for suggestions and feedback from colleagues. This shared accountability led to greater use of the innovations.

There are other ways that you can assure accountability for the use of professional development. They include an instructional walkthroughs organized and led by teachers, opportunities to examine student work samples, or lesson study activities. You might also ask for samples of student work, rather than solely looking at lesson plans. This allows you to see the end results of instruction: student performance. Tool 71-Accountability through Professional Development provides a planning guide.

Tool 71 My School's Plan for Accountability through Professional Development

Examples
◆ Teachers share one new idea they implemented at the first staff meeting following any professional development activity. Meet in small groups, share the idea, and ask for suggestions and feedback from colleagues.
◆ Conduct an instructional walkthrough or learning walk organized by teachers and focused on locating examples of the use of recent professional development.
◆ Create opportunities for teachers to look at student work samples (see www.lasw.org for meeting protocols).
◆ When visiting classrooms or talking with teachers, ask to see samples of student work rather than requesting to see lesson plans.
Plans for Our School:

What if...

"In the past, we haven't really done any follow-up for our professional development. How do I shift that perception?"

You begin by talking with your leadership team or school improvement team. You might ask people who recently attended a conference to share their learning at a faculty meeting. Or you might ask a team that participated in a recent workshop to demonstrate how to apply their learning. A principal we met in North Carolina asked grade level teams to work together to use the things they learned in professional development and monitoring the implementation.

Accountability through School Improvement

We suggest that you use your school improvement process to support your vision of a more rigorous school. Use Tool 72-Analysis of School Improvement Plan as a starting point to check its alignment with your work to improve the rigor of your school.

Tool 72   Analysis of School Improvement Plan

Locate a copy of your current school improvement plan and use it to respond to the following questions. Respond to each of the questions and use this scale: 1 – Strongly Disagree 3–Neutral 5 – Strongly Agree 2 – Disagree 4–Agree	Rating
1. Our vision for a more rigorous school is reflected in the plan.	
2. The plan was developed collaboratively with teachers, staff, students, families, and community.	
3. The goals in the plan help propel us toward becoming more rigorous.	
4. Resources (time, budget) are used to support achieving our goals.	
5. The plan clearly describes the set of indicators or data points we will use to measure our success.	
6. The plan includes a process for regular monitoring and adjusting to assure progress towards becoming more rigorous.	
Recommended Improvements:	

Tool 73 – Accountability For Families and Community

It is also important that families are provided with the information and tools they need to support your vision of a more rigorous school. We've found that families are almost always supportive of increasing the quality and rigor of their children's school. Often, however, they want specific ideas about how they can be helpful. Tool 73A-Ideas to Support Families describes practical ways you can support families.

Tool 73A   Ideas to Support Families

Examples
♦ Provide tips for how to organize the home to support completion of homework.
♦ Help families locate libraries and other helpful resources.
♦ Organize parent support groups.
♦ Create a parent library with books and materials about parenting and children's academic growth.
♦ Include tips for parents in every school newsletter.
♦ Arrange for parents to share ideas and strategies for supporting their child's success in school.

Tool 73B   My School's Plan to Support Families

Plans for Our School:

As part of your plan, you will want to regularly share information about your school, its program, and its successes with families. Using Tool 73C-Communicating with Families, build your plan.

Tool 73C   Communicating with Families

Examples
♦ Current data about student learning (test scores, major projects and assignments).   ♦ Awards and recognitions received by students and staff.   ♦ Stories about students who made a positive change in their learning.   ♦ Profiles of teachers who do "whatever it takes" to assure student success.
Our Plan:

What if...

"We focus on involving our parents and on communicating with them in a variety of ways. But it seems to be a one-way street. We are doing a lot of work, but we still don't get a sense of partnership from our parents. Shouldn't accountability go both ways?"

Accountability is a shared responsibility. But you can't use the response from parents as rationale for not continuing your efforts. Part of the problem may be that the school is always talking at parents rather than talking with parents. In addition to sharing information, gather information from parents about needs and interests. The Comer School Development Process suggests that you establish a parent council, separate from the PTO, that can provide you with advice about the best way to interact with parents. Schools can be intimidating places, particularly for people who may not have had a good experience in school. Work to make the school more inviting. Be sure your communications are written in plain English or Spanish, and don't use educational jargon.

Ensuring Accountability with Parents

Along with communication, it is important to help parents truly understand how they can appropriately help. For example, some parents are more knowledgeable about how to help their son or daughter with homework, others less so. As a result, some students do not receive any help at home; others receive too much. Tool 74-Homework Help Tips for Parents provide ideas for parents.

Tool 74   Homework Help Tips for Parents

+ Have a regular place for students to do homework. Ideally, it's well-lit, quiet, and tools are available (pencils, paper, etc.).

+ Establish a set time for homework and stick to it. This helps students learn time management.

+ Be careful not to provide too much help. It's fine to help, but if you answer for them, they can learn to quit and allow someone else to do the work instead.

+ If your student is frustrated, encourage, ask questions, and help . . . but again, don't do the work for them. This will teach them to persevere.

+ When your student asks, "Is this right?" ask them, "What do you think? Why?" This will encourage them to think for themselves and it will build self-confidence.

+ Be positive and participate. You can do your own "homework"—read a magazine while they are reading; pay bills while they are doing math.

Adapted from Homework Tips for Parents: *www2.ed.gov/parents/.../homework/homeworktips.pdf*

Often, we hear teachers and principals explain that they use written communications and parent signatures as a form of parent accountability. We ask parents to sign homework policies or student agendas in an effort to share accountability. But legally, those signatures don't mean much other than we notified parents of our policies. Parents cannot sign away their rights.

If you use written communication be sure it is written in plain English and avoids the use of educational jargon. You may have parents who will be unable to read the forms and won't know about the need to sign and return forms.

There are a wide range of strategies for communicating with families. We've provided a basic starting point, and included other ideas in Chapter Seven: Structures to Support Success.

Based on the examples and your own experiences, what strategies are you currently using that support student accountability?

_____

_____

_____

What other strategies would you like to implement?

_____

_____

_____

What if...

"What does this mean? Are you saying we shouldn't have parents sign policies or agendas?"

No. What we are saying is that isn't enough! In one of our recent workshops, a teacher commented that since parents sign off on his homework policies, then it becomes their responsibility to make sure the homework is completed. If not, it's an automatic zero. Parent signatures are not an excuse. We still need to communicate regularly with students and parents. We still need to provide support for students who are struggling. And we believe that automatic zeroes let students off the hook for learning rather than holding them to the high expectations of completing their work. We'll address this in the student accountability section of this chapter.

Accountability for Students

Students also share accountability for their own learning. Too often they are not included in efforts to increase rigor.

Students must be actively involved in their own learning by making decisions about their learning and by being responsible for asking questions, being clear about their work, and completing assignments.

Students also need to know the expectations for their work. Some of their most frequent questions include: What are the grading standards? Where do I go for additional support? How do I locate examples of high quality assignments? Where may I locate resources to complete my work? Tool 75-Ways to Support Student Accountability provides a list of examples of specific strategies you can use.

Tool 75   Ways to Support Student Accountability

Examples
◆ Provide exemplars for all work and rubrics that students can use to assess their success in completing assignments.
◆ Provide opportunities for students to revise and resubmit work.
◆ Include support and scaffolding in classroom instruction.
◆ Include engaging instructional activities connected to real life.
◆ Act consistently on the belief that each student can learn, will learn, and you have the power to help them do so.
◆ Provide quality and timely feedback on student work.

Plans for Our School:

Tool 76 – Rigor through Requiring Demonstration of Learning

One controversial aspect of rigor is grading. For a more thorough discussion of classroom grading policies, you may want to read Chapter Eight: Grading and Assessment in *Rigor is NOT a Four-Letter Word* (Blackburn, 2008). However, at this point, is important to consider one aspect of assessment and grading in our discussion of student accountability.

Too often, students don't complete work that requires a demonstration of learning. Typically, this results in a low grade. We often think this means students learn the importance of responsibility, but more often they learn that if they are willing to "take a lower grade or a zero," then they do not actually have to complete their work. For some, that is a preferable alternative to doing work. Perhaps they don't fully understand the assignment or they may not want to complete it. However, if we truly have high expectations for students, we don't let them off the hook for learning.

The use of a "Not Yet" or "Incomplete" policy for projects and assignments shifts the emphasis to learning and allows students to revise and resubmit work until it is at an acceptable level. Requiring quality work, work that meets the teachers expectations, lets students know that the priority is learning, not simple completion of an assignment.

Recently, we had the opportunity to speak with Toni Eubank of the Southern Regional Education Board (SREB). As part of their comprehensive school reform model, SREB has long been a proponent of holding students to high expectations for completed work. She describes the model as Instant Credit Recovery (or Instant Content Recovery for middle school students).

> This grading intervention practice requires that teachers rethink credit recovery completely. If it is okay for students to retake courses to meet standards, why is it not okay to retake tests that do not meet standards, revise essays, redo class-work and homework that do not meet standards? Why do we let students "off the hook" for learning and for completing work that meets the standards during our classes, and then spend thousands and thousands of dollars requiring them to *retake* entire courses they have failed, many simply because they did not do homework? Instead of sitting in classes throughout the semester or year putting forth little to no effort, doing little work, failing tests or turning in garbage instead of high-quality work, students must now be required to work as they go. This method truly reflects job-embedded skills and habits and better prepares students for college and careers. Instead of retaking courses and earning credit (often for seat time only) in our current credit recovery programs, students must now work while they go—sort of a "pay as you go" method. (Eubank, 2011, p. 1)

Tool 76A lists the Eight Key Elements of the Instant Credit Recovery Model (Eubank, 2011).

Tool 76A   Eight Key Elements of the Instant Credit Recovery Model

1. Teachers no longer assign grades below a C.

2. Eliminate the use of zeros.

3. Late work is late, but it must be completed if teachers are to correctly determine if students know, understand, and are able to do whatever the verb within the standard calls for.

4. Students must be given extra help opportunities (required) to learn the information, skill, or concept to complete assignments.

5. Students must retake tests that they fail and redo all assignments they earn less than a C grade on.

6. Consequences change for students not having work ready to turn in on time.

7. Grading systems change from zeros or failing grades to "I's" or some other form of non-grade.

8. A few students will still fail no matter what. The goal is to get MORE students to complete MORE assignments and assessments to the proficient level of the standard.

What if...

"Our school is one of the best in our area. Parents know we have high expectations, and if students don't do the work, they receive a zero. Some of our teachers are known for the high numbers of failures, but they are also some of the most requested teachers. Zeroes and failing grades prepare our students for real life."

The following response is quoted from Toni Eubank (SREB).

Life has many do-overs, and when teachers think otherwise, they do not have a handle on the "real world" as it works today. Quality is the most important component of any job. Ask BP oil workers, their supervisors and even their now defunct CEOs. When due dates and dollars replace high-quality work, or even minimum standards, the results can be devastating. America was built on quality and innovation, and until and unless we instill these values into our students, they leave our schools with notions about "the real world" that do not actually exist in their lives. When I hear things like, "they won't get to redo work when they get on the job. They will have timelines, and if they don't do the work, they will get fired." Actually, on the job, they will have a set of expectations and responsibilities that require them to do their work at high levels and they will have to redo that work until they get it right. If they are unable to do it to begin with, they will get extra help—a lot of extra help. If the job requires knowledge and skills they do not have, they will get on-the-job training, assistance and even a mentor until they are able to do the work. Some need longer training than others, but only the inept or lazy do not make it through. If they are still unable or unwilling, they will be notified of the need for improvement, usually more than once. In most jobs, they will get verbal, then written notification of the quality of their work and of what will need to happen in order to remain on the job. If they still do not meet the work standard, then and only then will those workers be fired. Few jobs require workers to do perfect, even high-quality, or even minimal work or be fired on the spot. There are steps in the firing process that must be followed.

Our current methods and the real values our schools teach students is the opposite of almost every real-world job. "If you don't do your work, you will get a zero," tells a student there is an *option* to do work or not. They can do the work *or* they can choose not to do the work. A zero is something that occurs in their future, and in this world, this generation works almost solely through instant gratification and instant consequences, students do not understand the impact of zeros, even when teachers try to tell them. (Eubank, 2011, p. 2–3)

Robin Madden, a teacher in Rock Hill, South Carolina, shares a pilot grading policy (Tool 76B-Sample Reassessment Policy) developed by teachers at Saluda Trail Middle School and South Pointe High School. It focuses on allowing students to revise summative and formative assignments for reassessment.

Tool 76B   Sample Reassessment Policy

♦ Students are provided at least one re-assessment opportunity per major task/assessment.

♦ When reassessment is offered, all students may be reassessed, regardless of the grade on the original task/assessment.

　　In other words, all students may re-take summative or formative assessments, as long as they re-learn the material first.

♦ Students who cheat are also allowed to re-take, but they're docked 20 percent and a written administrative referral.

♦ The reassessment grade should replace the original grade if it is higher than the original grade. Students are assigned the higher of the two grades.

Final Thoughts and Action Planning

There has been a significant shift in accountability in schools. The focus is clearly on the collective accountability of teachers and administrators for the success of every student. Each individual shares a personal responsibility and accountability for doing whatever it takes to assure student success.

Ultimately, it all begins and ends with each individual's personal vision for his or her school or classroom, commitment to increasing rigor, willingness to take risks, support others, work collaboratively, and abandon long-standing practices that are not successful.

Effective principals have a clear vision about how their school can improve. They work with teachers, families, and the community to implement the vision. But a school where rigorous learning occurs is more than just a vision, it is about shared responsibility for implementing the vision and shared accountability for the results.

As you work with your teachers, families, and community to support their efforts, it's important to help them recognize that improvement is a continuous process rather than a single event. How will you plan your next steps?

My Action Plan for Accountability

The most important tool from this chapter in my current situation is:

_____

_____

_____

_____

_____

_____

I also think the following concepts and/or tools would be useful in my situation:

_____

_____

_____

_____

_____

_____

_____

I need additional help or resources in the form of:

_____

_____

_____

_____

_____

_____

My next action steps are to:

_____

_____

_____

_____

_____

_____

_____

9

Structures
that Support Rigor

Throughout this book we've emphasized the importance of vision. Vision is critically important when working to become a more rigorous school. But visions without action to implement the vision are just words.

Structure can be either a barrier to reform or a way to accelerate the work. Effective principals recognize the power of structure to change their school. They know that collaborative time, design of teaching assignments, and priorities in the schedule significantly impact your ability to achieve your vision.

In this chapter we will discuss structures that support teachers, students, families, and leaders as they work to improve the rigor of their school. These tools will help you maintain momentum toward achieving your vision.

Tools in Chapter Nine: Structures that Support Rigor	
Tool 77	Options for Collaborative Teams
Tool 78	Assess Your Professional Learning Community
Tool 79	Providing Collaborative Time
Tool 80	Plan for Use of Collaborative Time
Tool 81	Sample School Scheduling Strategies
Tool 82	Using Your School's Schedule to Increase Rigor
Tool 83	Schedules that Support Improved Rigor
Tool 84	Providing Value and Success for Students
Tool 85	Options for Motivating Students
Tool 86	Structures to Provide Extra Support
Tool 87	Structures to Support Families
Tool 88	Structures to Support the Leader

Professional Learning Communities

Creating a professional learning community (PLC) is common in many schools. It is one way to work collaboratively to improve the rigor of your school and your classrooms. PLC's take many forms but are almost uniformly focused on improving student learning.

We've also found that many groups are called professional learning communities when they are not. This distorts the important role that PLC's play in focusing your efforts on improved student learning. We see PLC's as a structure that can create shared accountability. It is a structure that builds a shared commitment to important school goals. By using your PLC to look at data and monitor your progress, you can create greater accountability for improving rigor.

Successful professional learning communities provide time for teachers and others to meet, talk about curriculum and instruction, and examine data about student learning. The most vital aspect of this collaborative activity is that it provides time for people to meet, talk about rigor in their school and identify strategies for making their school more rigorous.

In Chapter Six we discussed the impact of professional learning communities as collaborative tools. We also provided a tool (Tool 43) that you can use to assess your own dispositions regarding professional learning communities. Here, we'll turn our focus on the structural aspects of PLCs.

There are many different types of collaborative teams. Tool 77-Options for Collaborative Teams can be used to determine which option best fits your needs.

The focus is on continuous improvement with a results orientation. One principal described it as a "laser light focus on getting the desired results."

Tool 77 Options for Collaborative Teams

Option	Description	How this option could address student learning needs	Advantages	Disadvantages
Faculty-wide teams	Participation of the entire faculty in teams focused on the same issue.			
Interdisciplinary teams	Teams across grade or content areas or that share common planning time or the same students.			
Grade-level teams	Focus on students at a single grade level.			
Vertical teams	Working together across grade levels.			
Subject-area teams	Focus within a single content area.			
Special topic teams	Teams formed around topics of interest.			
Between school teams	Teachers from different schools work together.			

Adapted from: *Team to Teach: A Facilitator's Guide to Professional Learning Teams.* National Staff Development Council, 2009.

Tool 78-Assess Your Professional Learning Community can be used to assess the current status of your professional learning communities. It can be used as a self-assessment or used with your School Improvement Team or other governance group. You might also use it at a staff meeting. Organize teachers into groups of four so that each group represents several grades and/or content areas. Ask each group to complete the assessment. Then share the results and use them to have a conversation about how to strengthen your work in this area.

Tool 78   Assess Your Professional Learning Community

Rate your professional learning communities using this scale:
 	
  1 – Strongly Disagree   3–Neutral   5 – Strongly Agree
  2 – Disagree   4–Agree
	Rating

1. We're organized into collaborative teams to work on curricular and instructional issues.	
2. Collaboration is embedded into our routine practice.	
3. We have agreed upon indicators or data points that we will use to measure our progress.	
4. We analyze student achievement data to help us establish goals for our work.	
5. We monitor the learning of each student so that we can monitor and adjust our work.	
6. We maintain a "laser light" focus on results.	
7. Each team member is clear about our goals, student expectations, and common assessments.	
8. We use the results of our assessments to identify students who need additional time or support and establish processes to assure that they get the support they need.	
9. We agree to and honor our commitments to members of our collaborative teams.	
10. Our collaboration is focused first on improving student learning.	
11. Our collaboration is also focused on teachers helping others improve.	
12. Our collaborative teams help us build shared knowledge about best practice.	
13. Our teams have established norms and protocols.	
14. Our teams maintain a focus on team goals.	
15. Our collaborative work is monitored and supported.	

What if...

"Who should complete this? Should this be a tool for my own self-reflection or should I also give it out to my faculty?"

You can use it several ways. We think you should use it to reflect on your own school. But you can also use it with your leadership team or school improvement team, or with your entire faculty. Of course, you only want to use it with your faculty if your school has worked to create collaborative groups and a professional learning community.

Time for Collaboration

An essential component of professional learning communities is time for teachers to work with colleagues on professional tasks. We've found that collaborative time is one of the catalysts for nurturing and sustaining change. Teachers value the opportunity to meet with grade or content peers to discuss successes, diagnose ways to improve, and develop a repertoire of strategies that they can use in their own classrooms.

There are many different ways to provide collaborative time. They vary considerably depending on the grade level of the school. Tool 79-Providing Collaborative Time describes some of the most common methods and providing an opportunity for you to reflect on possible options for your school.

What if...

"How much time should be provided for collaborative planning?"

The amount of time will vary depending on the task, but we've learned that less frequent extended blocks of time are more useful and more productive than more frequent short periods of time. Too often, collaborative time is time taken away from regular planning. In elementary school, students may be at a special class, while in middle and high school teachers may use a scheduled planning period. While better than nothing, these time are often far less productive because teachers are attending to other professional tasks.

Tool 79   Providing Collaborative Time

Strategy	Description
Common Planning	When teachers share a common planning period, they may use some of the time for collaborative work.
Parallel Scheduling	Special teachers (PE, music, art, etc.) are scheduled so that grade level or content area teachers have common planning.
Shared Classes	Teachers in more than one grade or team combine their students into a single large class for specific instruction and the other teachers can collaborate.
Faculty Meeting	Find other ways to communicate the routine items shared during faculty meetings and reallocate that time to collaborative activities.
Adjust Start or End of Day	Members of a team, grade, or entire school agree to start their workday early or extend their workday one day a week to gain collaborative time.
Late Start or Early Release	Adjust the start or end of the school day for students and use the time for collaborative activity.
Professional Development Days	Rather than traditional large group professional development, use the time for teams of teachers to engage in collaborative work.

Ways We Currently Provide Collaborative Time:

What IS Working with our Collaborative Time:

What IS NOT Working with our Collaborative Time:

Adapted from Williamson (2009) and DuFour, DuFour, Eaker & Many (2006)

What if...

"We have collaborative time, but it's not used effectively in my view. Teachers want to use it for their own purposes and parents think our early release days are a waste of time."

Schools that have collaborative time are lucky. So that the district isn't tempted to take the time away, it is important to use the time productively. We've learned from principals that the most important thing you can do is be very specific about the task that is to be completed during collaborative time. There needs to be a product expected from each work group and then you need to monitor the use of the time. The best way to do that is to pop in on meetings to be part of the collaboration and to get a sense of what is working and what is not.

Ron has negotiated lots of teacher contracts and parents resist early release days because it messes with daycare and family work schedules. Always work to develop a schedule that doesn't infringe on parents' lives.

We've also learned that the greatest collaboration occurs when there is an opportunity for extended work together. That occurs best in half-day or full-day sessions, rarely in an hour of early release. At the end of the day, teachers are tired and it is difficult to commit to a task knowing that you have only limited time for completion.

Tool 80 – Plan for Use of Collaborative Time

Regardless of the way you provide time for collaboration, the most important thing is how you use the time. It is important that it be productive and supports your vision of improved rigor. Tool 80A-Examples of Collaborative Tasks provides options for your consideration; Tool 80B-Action Plan for Collaborative Time allows you to create your own plan.

TOOL 80A   Examples of Collaborative Tasks

- ◆ Meet in vertical teams to work on articulation of the curriculum
- ◆ Work with grade level teachers to examine student work
- ◆ Talk with the School Improvement Team about conducting walkthroughs or learning walks focused on rigor
- ◆ Conduct a book study on *Rigor is Not a Four-Letter Word* or *Rigorous Schools and Classrooms: Leading the Way*

Tool 80B   Action Plan for Collaborative Time

Component	Changes to Be Made
When It Is Available	
Who Participates	
How the Time is Used	
Other	

Organizing to Promote Collaboration

Many schools use their schedule to provide collaborative time. There are many different ways to organize the schedule (Williamson, 2009), but some provide more opportunity for collaboration than others.

Tool 81-Sample School Scheduling Strategies describes the ways we've found most effective at providing opportunity for teachers to collaborate. We've grouped them into elementary and secondary examples, but many of the strategies work in both settings.

Of course, none of these models assure that teachers will collaborate, but they do provide the structure and the opportunity. We've found that these structures are more likely to be used if teachers are involved in selecting the model. Once the structure is in place it is important to encourage its use. One way to provide encouragement is for you, as the leader, to attend and participate when teachers meet during collaborative time. Be careful not to take over the meeting. But your presence is a visual reminder of the importance of meeting.

Tool 81 Sample School Scheduling Strategies

Elementary School Examples

Strategy	Description
Location of Classrooms	A common way to promote collaboration is to locate all early elementary classes on the same floor or in the same wing. Similarly, all the later elementary classes can be located near one another. One principal we met said that it "allowed each wing to focus on the developmental issues with their students" and "promoted collaboration among grade-level teachers."
Scheduling Special Classes	Schedule special classes such as music, art, and physical education so that teachers at a single grade or combination of grades have common planning.
Parallel Scheduling	At each grade level, one or two teachers might specialize in math and science and one or two others specialize in reading, language arts, and social studies. By organizing all the teachers at a grade level so that they have a similar schedule, including when students go to special classes, you create time each day when those teachers can meet and collaborate.

Secondary School Examples

Strategy	Description
Teaming	Teams consist of a group of teachers who share students and often have common planning time to meet and talk about curricular and instructional issues.
School Within-a-School	One way to respond to the anonymity present in large schools is to organize into smaller units, often called houses or small schools within a school. In such a model, students and teachers often remain in the same unit for most of the day.
Organization of Curricular Departments	Group curricular departments together rather than maintaining a separate organization. They can share office space and be expected to work collaboratively on curriculum design, interdisciplinary links, and instructional improvement.
Common Planning for Teachers in a Single Course or Combination of Courses	Arrange the schedule so that teachers of a single course, or combination of courses, share a planning period. The time can be used to design common assessments that can be used to measure student success. Common planning provides an opportunity to work collaboratively to redesign lessons that were less effective than desired and to re-enforce practices that contributed to student success.

Ideas for Providing Collaborative Time:

_____

_____

_____

_____

_____

_____

_____

_____

_____

_____

_____

_____

_____

_____

Tool 82 – Using Your School's Schedule to Increase Rigor

Your school's schedule is a powerful tool to improve rigor and provide teachers with the tools they need to implement your shared vision of a more rigorous school. Too often, the emphasis is on the logistics of the schedule. We've found that the most effective leaders see the schedule as a tool that can be used to positively impact their instructional program.

You can use your schedule to provide collaborative time for teachers to work together on improving rigor. They can focus on instructional strategies, ways to provide additional support for students, or steps to provide more interdisciplinary or in-depth instruction.

TOOL 82A   What We Know About School Schedules

♦ Schedules reflect a school's values and priorities.

♦ The most effective schedules are anchored in a shared vision.

♦ A quality schedule emerges when teachers and administrators work together to establish priorities and select a design.

♦ Without clear goals, the schedule is merely a plan for organizing teachers and students; when guided by goals, the schedule becomes a powerful tool to positively impact teaching and learning.

From: Williamson (2009)

The first step is to talk with your teachers about the schedule. A shared vision and clarity of purpose helps build support for the schedule. For example, you might want to talk with your School Improvement Team about the schedule and how it might support your vision of a rigorous school.

Organize the conversation around a series of questions designed to promote thinking and generate ideas. The questions in Tool 82B-Starting a Conversation About the Schedule serve to organize their thinking and keep the discussion focused.

Tool 82B   Starting a Conversation About the Schedule

Examples of Questions
◆ How do we allocate time to content areas based on student need? ◆ What are ways that we can create longer instructional blocks and provide regular time for teacher's to collaborate? ◆ How do we provide flexibility so that we can give the students who need extra time or support the help they need? ◆ How will each option provide opportunity for greater depth in the curriculum? ◆ How will the scheduling options allow us to increase rigor in instructional activities? ◆ What options do we have for greater interdisciplinary instruction?
Questions We Might Use at Our School:

Regardless of the plan, we've found that building support among those responsible for implementing any change is important. Talk openly about every option. Discuss the advantages and disadvantages. Communicate with stakeholders and provide an opportunity for them to provide suggestions and input. You'll find other tools you can use to build ownership in other chapters.

What if...

"Changing a schedule is a big deal in our school, and any change must be justified based on our test scores."

Changing any schedule is a big deal because the schedule is so directly related to workload and allocation of resources. Rather than focus on test scores, we suggest you focus on improving instruction, which will improve test scores. Work with your faculty to examine how you use time and how it might be reallocated to improve instructional quality. For example, many secondary schools benefit from having longer blocks of time. The longer time periods don't need to occur every day, but their existence means that teachers can plan for lessons that may involve different instructional practices.

Finally, there is no research to show that schedule is linked to test scores. However, there is evidence that a more flexible use of time can impact teacher instruction, student learning, and student engagement, all factors that tend to positively impact student learning.

Tool 83 – Schedules that Support Improved Rigor

There are many different kinds of schedules with all sorts of variations. All have advantages and disadvantages and reflect values about the use of time, opportunity for collaboration, and the importance of providing additional support for students. If you consider changing your schedule, you will want to talk about the options and select the model that will be most helpful achieving your vision of a more rigorous school.

We want to be very clear, however. Your schedule is just a tool that creates a structure to improve rigor. The most important issue is how the time is used. Merely using the time to increase coverage will not improve rigor.

Tool 83A   Sample Schedules

Type of Schedule	Description
Block	Block schedules provide long instructional blocks that teachers can use for greater instructional flexibility. Block schedules often release energy and creativity among teachers when they know they are not bound by a fixed period schedule.
4 x 4 Block	Many high schools have also adopted a block schedule commonly called a four-by-four block. In such a schedule, each class is longer and fewer classes meet each day. At some schools, the classes alternate from day to day. At others, the classes meet daily and change at the end of the semester. The four-by-four block schedule allows teachers to design lessons with opportunity for more in-depth instruction, time for guided practice, and more time to monitor student learning.
Alternating Day	In this schedule, classes do not meet every day but alternate every other day. Alternating schedules may provide longer blocks of time for classes and are often used to provide an opportunity for students to take additional classes. Some schools use the alternating day schedule as a way to provide time for additional instruction or other supports for students. Below is an example of an alternating schedule.
Trimester	In the trimester schedule, the school year is divided into three equal parts with courses scheduled accordingly. The ability for a student who fails a class to "recover" more quickly is one of the major advantages of a trimester model. In a traditional schedule, a student might need to wait a full year before being able to retake a class. With the trimester model, the student can repeat the class more quickly the next trimester. Some classes may meet one trimester, some two, and some even all three trimesters. Generally, each class period is longer than in a traditional schedule and most classes meet only one trimester.

It is often helpful to assess your current schedule to see whether it supports or inhibits achieving your vision of a more rigorous school. Tool 83B-Assess Your School's Schedule from *The Principalship from A to Z* (Williamson & Blackburn, 2009) is a helpful tool for conducting such an assessment.

Tool 83B   Assess Your School's Schedule

	High	**Medium**	**Low**
Participation	Teachers are actively involved in selecting the design of the schedule.	Limited involvement of some teachers in design of the schedule.	Teachers are not involved in selecting the design of the schedule.
Decision Making	The adoption of a new schedule design is made using an agreed upon decision-making process.	The decision-making process involves some teachers and other school personnel.	Adoption of a new schedule is problematic because it was decided by the administration.
Use of Data	Multiple sources of data including data about student learning are used to guide selection of a new schedule design.	Limited data are used to establish the design of the schedule.	Little or no data is gathered and used to guide decisions about the design of the school schedule.
Professional Development	A multiyear professional development program focused on instructional design supports adoption of a new schedule.	Some professional development is provided.	No professional development is provided to support adoption of a new schedule.
Long Instruction Blocks	The school day provides long instructional blocks that can be used to meet the instructional needs of students.	The schedule includes some instructional blocks in some subjects.	Instructional time is divided into fixed period classes that minimize options for flexible instructional practices.
Presence of Common Planning Time	The schedule provides common time during the school day for teachers who work together to meet and plan instruction.	Some teachers have common planning time with other teachers at their grade or in their content area.	The schedule provides little or no common planning time for teachers who share students or teach a common grade or content area.
Grouping and Regrouping	Teachers may group or regroup students within grades or teams to address individual learning needs.	The schedule provides limited opportunity to group and regroup students.	The organization of teachers and classes inhabits the regrouping of students for instruction.
Use of Space	Individual teachers or teaching teams make decisions about the use of their instructional time.	Some flexibility is built into the schedule for teachers to allocate instructional time.	The schedule does not allow teachers to flexibly use classroom instructional time.

Structures for Motivating Students

We believe that an essential part of improving rigor is the importance of expecting students to learn at high levels and supporting each student so that he or she can learn. Structures to support students are essential to becoming a more rigorous school.

When we work in schools, we are always reminded of the importance of motivating students to do well in school and supporting their success. We're told repeatedly about students who come to class with few materials, no books, and a lackluster attitude. In her book *Classroom Motivation from A to Z* (2005), Barbara provides many examples of ways to motivate students and engage them in learning. For now, here are several important things about motivation.

Two things, value and success, are the keys to intrinsic motivation for every student. Value is whether the person sees value in what they are doing. Success is whether or not they believe they will be successful and feel successful.

Value – Find ways to link what students are learning to things in their own lives and to things they find useful.

Success – Every one of us is motivated by success. Too often our students have not experienced success and have learned to become disengaged. It's just not enough for the teacher to tell students they can be successful. They must experience success. Therefore, it is important to design lessons and assignments where students can be successful. We must support students and allow them to experience success so that they can build on that experience in other settings.

Use Tool 84-Providing Value and Success for Students to reflect on the ways your teachers currently provide value and build success. What are other options you might try?

Tool 84   Providing Value and Success for Students

Ideas for Providing Value	Ideas for Building Success

It is also helpful to ask teachers to consider these two aspects when planning a lesson. For example, in order to ensure value, teachers can consider, "How does this lesson answer a student's question, 'Why do I need to know this?'" To address success, how does the teacher address differentiation for the learners in his or her classroom? How does he or she provide support, and how does a student receive extra help, if needed?

Many schools adopt programs that help to extrinsically motivate students. Tool 85-Options for Motivating Students provides examples as well as an opportunity to assess your school.

Tool 85   Options for Motivating Students

Example

Student Rewards Program: Students who meet identified goals (grades, organization, attendance, service) earn points redeemable for a reward each quarter or semester.

Student Recognition Program: During class observations or as a result of work in class, teachers or administrators can recognize students. Being recognized can qualify you for a weekly raffle for an award.

Academic Success Time: The schedule can be organized to provide time during the school day to assist students struggling in a content area.

Assess Your School:

Current programs:

_____

_____

_____

_____

_____

_____

_____

Ideas of programs to consider:

_____

_____

_____

_____

_____

_____

_____

_____

Tool 86 – Structures to Provide Extra Support

There are lots of great ideas for providing extra help and support to students. Barry Knight, Principal of Palmetto Middle School in Anderson, SC, provided many of the examples included in Tool 86-Structures to Provide Extra Support.

Tool 86   Structures to Provide Extra Support

Examples of Ways to Provide Extra Support:

Lunch Time Learning – A center that is open every day during lunch to provide academic support to students.

LIFT (Letting Individuals Fine-Tune) – Each Wednesday during related arts classes, students who need additional instruction to reach mastery are required to meet with their academic teachers for additional small group instruction.

Rock'nRAP – Teachers assist students with research work and encourage reading newspapers and magazines with music creating an inviting atmosphere.

21st Century Learning Center – Provides healthy snacks, supervised recreational activity, homework assistance, and special learning programs for students after school. Bus transportation is provided.

IMAX – **Initiative to Maximize Academic Excellence** – A school-wide approach to keep learning going and to help students succeed who are comfortable with failure. At the end of each month (exact date a secret), students with no Incompletes are awarded a treat for their diligence completing schoolwork (ice cream, music, fruit, free time, coupons to school store, or tickets to events). Students with Incompletes remain with their academic teachers to finish their work.

Reorganize the Schedule – A Michigan school changed their schedule so that two seminar periods were scheduled each week. The seminars provided time for students to get extra help from teachers, revise and resubmit assignments, or receive additional instruction.

Use Lunch/Advisory Time – In Tucson, a high school principal reorganized the day so that twice a week the lunch period was extended, allowing students to retake tests, work in the study lab, or meet with individual teachers about missing assignments.

Things We're Current Doing to Provide Extra Support:

_____

_____

_____

_____

Things We Might Consider:

_____

_____

_____

_____

Tool 87 – Structures to Support Families

Families are essential partners in your work to become a more rigorous school. In other chapters we've discussed the importance of working with families and ways you can gain their support for your vision of a more rigorous school, but we want to emphasize that you will want to create structures that provide families with the knowledge and tools about how they can support the school's work and their child's success. Tool 87-Structures to Support Families contains suggestions and an opportunity to reflect.

Tool 87 Structures to Support Families

Examples of Ways to Support Families:

Provide Frequent Communication – Use multiple methods to share information with families about your school's vision of increased rigor. Consider use of traditional methods like newsletters but also use of social media like your school's website or school *Facebook* account.

Organize a Forum – Arrange to hold a forum at a time convenient to families where they can talk with other families and share ideas about how they support the success of their students.

Arrange Workshops – Provide parents with workshops on topics of interest that will support your agenda of increased rigor. For many high school parents. there is a need for information about college entrance requirements and access to financial aid.

Family Friendly Website – Create a website or add a parent/family page to your current site. Provide access to resources about family activities that support success in school (meals, sleep, quiet time for homework, place to do homework) and local community resources like free or low-cost dental and health care, nutrition information, and parks and recreation department activities. Make it your parents' one-stop site for up-to-date information about your school and resources helpful to families.

Things We're Currently Doing to Support Families:

_____

_____

_____

_____

_____

Things We Might Consider:

_____

_____

_____

_____

_____

Tool 88 – Structures to Support the Leader

Leaders also need support. It is essential for leaders to have take time to reflect on their own work, process their own learning, and consider how they can refine what they are doing to improve the rigor of their school. Take the time to consider the examples in Tool 88-Supporting Yourself as a Leader and reflect on which would help you.

Tool 88   Supporting Yourself as a Leader

Examples of Support	Way This Option Could Support My Work to Lead a More Rigorous School
Identify a coach or mentor who you can talk with about your work. Good coaches enable leaders to process their learning and to step back and reflect on how they might improve their work.	
Stay current in the field by reading voraciously and attending conferences and other professional development activities.	
Find time to meet with colleagues to share ideas and think about how you can support one another's efforts.	
Join your professional association and access its newsletters, journals, and other materials.	
My Plan for Supporting Myself as a Leader:	

Final Thoughts and Action Planning

The organization and structure of your school is one of your most powerful tools for shaping your school's program. It is critical to recognize the connection between the structures—the way you use time, arrangements for collaboration, and opportunity for sustained discussion of student learning—and achieving our vision. What structures will be part of your action plan?

My Action Plan for Creating Structures to Sustain Success

The most important tool from this chapter in my current situation is:

_____

_____

_____

_____

_____

I also think the following concepts and/or tools would be useful in my situation:

_____

_____

_____

_____

_____

I need additional help or resources in the form of:

_____

_____

_____

_____

_____

My next action steps are to:

_____

_____

_____

_____

_____

10

Moving Forward for Growth

Throughout this book we've talked about rigor, shared our definition, and discussed ways you can work with your school community to improve the rigor of your school and classrooms. Our focus has been on providing leaders with a set of tools. Like most toolboxes, there are several different tools. Not every tool works on every problem or in every school.

You will want to think about your school and select the tools that will work best in your setting. One of the things we've learned is that most jobs require more than one tool; at times, we find ourselves going back to our toolbox to select another tool because one didn't work exactly the way we thought it would. That's why we provided multiple tools in each chapter.

The tools in this book are designed to work together, as a package. Although you can choose to focus on one point of our COMPASS model, such as managing data, your efforts will be most successful when you develop a more comprehensive plan. For example, while managing data you will want to build ownership of the data and work collaboratively so that everyone shares accountability for using the data to improve student learning.

The most successful schools are those that recognize that they are constantly changing. The shifting demographic and social, economic, and political issues in our nation shape its schools. As a result, schools change a little each day in response to state and national standards, new research on student learning, and parent and community expectations.

The journey to becoming a more rigorous school is not straight, but winding. You will find yourself covering the same road twice, looping back on yourself, or even heading down an unknown road. To successfully navigate the road, you need a good set of tools, including a good COMPASS.

Tools in Chapter Ten: Moving Forward for Growth	
Tool 89	Supporting Teachers and Staff
Tool 90	Strategies for Dealing with Resistance
Tool 91	Concerns-Based Adoption Model
Tool 92	Assessing Needs
Tool 93	Have a Clear, Concrete Result
Tool 94	Celebrate Success
Tool 95	Assess Your Own Commitment
Tool 96	Change Attitudes
Tool 97	Self-Assessment of Focus on Students

Overcoming Resistance

When we work with schools, we often recognize that one of the biggest roadblocks to improving instructional rigor is the resistance from teachers, students, parents, or other building and district leaders. We recognize that every person deals differently with change. Some are more accepting, others more resistant. You may even find that at this point, even you are resistant to some of the needed changes. The tools in this section will help you and your school move beyond resistance to a focus on growth.

People often resist change because they are anxious about being accountable for results. Successful leaders understand that the success of any initiative is directly related to developing the capacity of the people in the organization to implement the change.

Tool 89 – Supporting Teachers and Staff

There are a variety of strategies to support your teachers and staff. Tool 89- Supporting Teachers and Staff will assist you as you plan which strategies will be most helpful.

TOOL 89 Supporting Teachers and Staff

Successful Strategies for Supporting Teachers and Staff	My Plans
1. Allow people to discuss feelings of loss and the difficulty of "letting go" of familiar programs and practices.	
2. Identify the needs of individuals and tailor support based on need.	
3. Develop support groups that focus on problem-solving and are non-judgmental.	
4. Be candid about unmet needs and work with people to plan specific ways to meet the needs.	
5. Focus on strengths, skills, and interests of each person.	
6. Provide opportunities for everyone to share their ideas and talents.	
7. Plan ways that individuals can expand their skills to support the innovation.	
8. Develop professional development tailored to each individual implementing the plan.	
9. Identify ways that individuals can work to support one another throughout the implementation.	
10. Focus on success and achievement.	
11. Provide extra support to those who need it.	
12. Keep communication open, positive, and encouraging.	

Adapted from: Gold and Roth (1999)

Resistance from Stakeholders

One of the biggest challenges you will face is the resistance that emerges from teachers, students, and families. This may be a good time to revisit Tool 38B-Force Field Analysis Form to reflect of the possible challenges from these stakeholders. There are five strategies that you can use to deal with resistance.

Tool 90   Strategies for Dealing with Resistance

1. Understand the resistance.

2. Have a clear, concrete result.

3. Check your own commitment.

4. Work to change attitudes.

5. Focus and refocus the conversation on students.

Understand the Resistance

Not everyone who resists increasing rigor does so because of ulterior motives. Often there is a conflict between their personal beliefs and values and the proposed changes. Their motives may be driven by concern for students, not outright resistance to an idea.

While some people resist just to resist, most people don't react that way. They are genuinely concerned about the proposed change. They either don't see the value in the change or they have concerns about how successful the change will be.

Tool 91 – Concerns-Based Adoption Model

The Southwest Educational Development Lab developed a way of monitoring change efforts. They created the Concerns-Based Adoption Model (CBAM) (Hord, Rutherford, Huling-Austin & Hall, 1987) and identified seven stages of concern. The CBAM model recognizes that change is complex and individuals experience change differently. Some people will readily embrace the change while others will have minimal awareness. Tool 91-Concerns-Based Adoption Model can be used to identify the variety of concerns in your school.

Again, the CBAM Model is an excellent tool to help you identify those factors that work for or against an innovation. We'd recommend that you reflect on the Force Field Analysis you completed in Tool 38B and make needed changes based on this new information.

Tool 91   Concerns-Based Adoption Model

CBAM Stages of Concern	Examples of Concern	Status in My School
6 Refocusing	What else can we do to improve rigor? How can I make my classroom even more rigorous?	
5 Collaboration	I'm pleased with my efforts to improve rigor, but I wonder what others have done.	
4 Consequence	Now that I've increased rigor, how am I doing? What evidence do I have that it is helping my students?	
3 Management	How can I develop the skills to create a more rigorous classroom? How can I do this with everything else I have to do?	
2 Personal	How will increasing rigor impact me? What will my plan to improve rigor look like?	
1 Informational	How do you increase rigor in your classroom? Where do I get information?	
0 Awareness	What is rigor? Things are fine; I'm not concerned about it.	

Adapted From: Hord, Rutherford, Huling-Austin & Hall, 1987

It is important for leaders to recognize participants' diverse feelings and concerns when you begin to work on improving rigor. Each individual will progress through the stages in a developmental manner. Not everyone will move at the same pace or have the same intensity of feeling.

Personal concerns (awareness, informational, personal) often characterize the first stage of your effort. As you begin to implement your plans, management concerns emerge. Once you are underway, teachers become more interested in the effects of rigor on students and on their classrooms.

What if…

"I've tried everything, but I have one teacher who continues to resist anything I suggest. How can I handle someone who won't cooperate, no matter what?"

Once you've tried everything you can do to get their cooperation, this becomes an administrative issue. There are tools available to principals. First, talk with the person so that you are absolutely clear about your expectations for cooperation. Second, never shirk your responsibility to accurately reflect their performance in personnel evaluations. In the narrative, factually describe how they fail to work collaboratively with others or fail to participate in professional development. Third, you can also minimize their influence by not including them on the school improvement team or other important work groups. Finally, you can choose to provide financial support for conference attendance and other professional development activities to those who support your vision.

Tool 92 – Assessing Needs

We've found that people resist change for two primary reasons. They don't see the value of the change, or they're unsure about how successful they will be with the change. Some of the most significant resistance comes when changing long-standing practices like grading. For example, we often find intense resistance to the idea of a "Not Yet" grading policy. Teachers may anticipate that it will be cumbersome to implement. Parents may worry that it doesn't hold kids accountable. School leaders may be concerned about explaining it to parents and community members.

We continue to find Maslow's hierarchy (1986) a useful way to think about what happens to people when they are asked to change. Under change-related stress, people may move to a lower level on the hierarchy. With support they are able to move to higher levels. Using Tool 92A-Assessing Needs of Teachers, consider the needs of your faculty.

Tool 92A   Assessing Needs of Teachers

Needs Identified by Maslow	Examples	Needs at My School
Aesthetic Need (self-actualization)	How do I focus first on the needs of students? How do I focus on my own learning?	
Need for Understanding *Need for Knowledge*	What do I need to know to be successful? What opportunities will I have for professional growth? What models exists that can help me plan a more rigorous classroom?	
Esteem Needs *Belonging Needs*	Will I be successful changing instruction? Will others value my work? How do the new norms around rigor align with my own beliefs?	
Security Needs *Survival Needs*	What will I be teaching? Will I have sufficient materials? Will I be able to provide a more rigorous educational experience for students? Who's making these decisions?	

Adapted from Maslow (1968) & Williamson & Blackburn (2010)

Tool 92B Assessing Needs of Stakeholders

Needs Identified by Maslow	Examples		
	Students	Families	Leaders
Aesthetic (self-actualization)	Focus on their own learning first.	First priority is supporting child's success.	Every action supports success for every student.
Need for Understanding *Need for Knowledge*	Will I have the knowledge to be successful? What level of support will I have?	Do I have the information to support my child's success? What examples are available to help me support my child?	Do I have the knowledge and skills to work with teachers, students, and families to improve rigor?
Esteem Needs *Belonging Needs*	Will I be successful? What will others think of me if I work hard?	Will I be successful changing family habits about homework?	What will other school leaders think of my work on this effort?
Security Needs *Survival Needs*	What happens if I am unsuccessful? Do I have the knowledge and skills for success?	What happens if my child and I disagree about the importance of school work?	Will my school be successful? Do I have the knowledge and skills to sustain our efforts to improve rigor?

Adapted from Maslow (1968) & Williamson & Blackburn (2010)

Of course, it's not just teachers who deal with the complexities of change. It also affects students, families, and leaders. Tool 92B-Assessing Needs of Stakeholders, provides examples of the varying needs for students, families, and leaders.

What if...

"Thinking about our situation through Maslow's viewpoint was helpful. But what if there are needs that I can't address?"

Sometimes you can't meet every need, but you may be able to link the person with the resources that might be helpful. We've found that most of the concern among teachers falls in the bottom three categories (safety/survival, esteem/belonging, understanding/knowledge). The best thing you can do is to make decisions about workload and teaching assignments (safety/security) as early as possible. Then recognize that professional development (understanding/knowledge) is not a one-time event. Many teachers don't have real questions about an innovation until they are actually implementing it. Create collaborative teams (esteem/belonging) that will work together to implement and monitor implementation. Finally, recognize that because we are individuals, people will need different things as they move forward.

Tool 93 – Have a Clear, Concrete Result

People often resist because they don't have a clear idea about what increased rigor will look like. They want to see a clear, defined outcome. You can overcome this resistance by providing a clear, concrete result. You should always be able to describe what success looks like. For example, "If we are successful implementing _____, we will know it because we will see _____."

We believe that you should not develop this in isolation. Work with your school improvement team to clearly articulate the vision and the outcomes. You should always be able to provide an explicit, measurable result. The examples in Tool 93A-Examples of Clear, Concrete Results may assist you as you develop your own statement in Tool 93B-Clear, Specific Outcome for Your School.

TOOL 93A   Examples of Clear, Concrete Results

- ◆ Teachers will use more analysis and synthesis questions with students.
- ◆ Students will be able to describe ways that they are supported in their work.
- ◆ Students, teachers, and families can discuss ways that student work samples have changed.
- ◆ Teachers can explain how classroom routines have been modified to provide time for students to revise and resubmit work.

Tool 93B   Clear, Specific Outcome for Your School

At this school, when we are successful increasing rigor, we will know it because we will see...

_____

_____

_____

_____

_____

_____

Tool 94 – Celebrate Success

Throughout the school improvement progress, it's important to celebrate your successes—both large and small. This is particularly true when progress seems limited. It's an excellent way to encourage all stakeholders to persist and persevere. Build celebrations into your culture.

Tool 94   Ways to Celebrate Success

- ◆ Recognize students who make progress.
- ◆ Recognize teachers who try something new.
- ◆ Surprise teachers with a note in their mailboxes.
- ◆ Identify "Students of the Month" and provide an outdoor picnic lunch.
- ◆ Provide a duty-free lunch for teachers. Use tablecloths, china, and decorations to make it special.
- ◆ Create a special brochure about the school and share it with business partners and other stakeholders.

Tool 95 – Assess Your Own Commitment

If you are not clear about your own commitment, it will become evident to others in your school. Teachers and families look to you, as the leader, for guidance. It's Leadership 101. What you pay attention to becomes important. Tool 95-Assess Your Own Commitment will help you reflect.

Tool 95   Assess Your Own Commitment

Do these describe you as a leader? Use this scale: 1 – Strongly Disagree 3–Neutral 5 – Strongly Agree 2 – Disagree 4–Agree	Rating
I'm open to new ideas and suggestions for improving rigor in my school.	
I'm enthusiastic about increasing rigor.	
I'm an active and enthusiastic learner.	
I participate in professional development with my teachers and staff.	
I am an attentive participant in professional development.	
I talk with teachers about ways to improve rigor in their classrooms.	
I visit classrooms specifically to observe and learn about our work to improve rigor.	
I model the use of good instruction in meetings and during other work with teachers.	

What if...

"I want to be committed, but I'm just tired. My staff is disheartened, and so am I."

Take time to celebrate your work together and celebrate your success. It is really important to celebrate small wins frequently. It's all about "success breeding success." Celebrating small gains on a regular basis can motivate teachers and students. Over time, these small gains add up to real growth.

Occasionally, people are just worn out. Take time to step back and reflect on your work together. You may want to pause briefly. Use one of your meetings to celebrate. Of course, refreshments make the celebration better. A principal we met in Montana asked his teachers to devote their weekend at least once a month to things they really enjoyed like biking, hiking, reading, or fishing. He told us that these interludes provided opportunities for people to recharge, and they almost always came back more energized than before.

Tool 96 – Change Attitudes

Positive attitudes are critical to the success of your plans to increase rigor. A positive attitude is a prerequisite for real improvements. Our attitudes come from our life experiences. They are learned. We develop them from dealing with family members, trying new things, and talking with persuasive or influential people. Because of these origins, our attitudes are individual and personal: each individual's attitude is unique.

Information alone is rarely enough to change anyone's attitude, but psychologists have identified three approaches to changing attitudes: cognitive, behavioral, and social.

Tool 96A   Approaches to Attitude Change

♦ Cognitive approaches focus on changing the way people think about something like rigor. This is frequently done by sharing information or using persuasive communication.

♦ Behavioral approaches use rewards and punishments. Since most people repeat behaviors that are rewarded and avoid those that are punished, such an approach can ultimately be used to shape beliefs about rigor.

♦ Social approaches rely on our tendency to do things like people we admire. We are more likely to copy their beliefs and behaviors. Providing examples of respected teachers with rigorous classrooms is an example of this approach.

Which of the three approaches (cognitive, behavioral, or social) is most common in your school and/or school district? Do you think it is the most effective?

_____
_____
_____
_____
_____
_____
_____
_____
_____

There are things that a leader can do to change the attitudes and beliefs of those with whom he or she works. Cognitive dissonance is the uncomfortable feeling we get when we recognize that something we believe to be true may not be. As soon as people become aware of the dissonance, they must reduce it.

New information often produces cognitive dissonance. It forces us to respond in one of three ways: deny the information, alter our behavior, or alter or rationalize our beliefs.

Tool 96B-Changing Attitudes uses these three approaches to provide an example of a plan for changing attitudes and beliefs about instructional rigor.

TOOL 96B   Changing Attitudes

Approach	Examples	Other Ideas for My School
Cognitive Approaches	• Share data about ways to improve rigor. • Provide professional development and other resources about rigor. • Share evidence of successful rigorous classrooms.	
Behavioral Approaches	• Provide training and instructional resources for teachers implementing greater rigor. • Provide additional released time for teachers to work with colleagues on instructional strategies for improving rigor.	
Social Approaches	• Establish mentor/buddy teams among teachers working on rigor. • Showcase practices used by teachers to increase rigor. • Provide an opportunity for testimonials about the success of increasing rigor at staff meetings.	

Focus and Refocus on Students

The importance of focusing on students seems so obvious. But we've found that when complex and difficult issues arise, student interests often become secondary to the interests of teachers, parents, or community. One part of the problem is that people describe everything they want to do as being "in the best interests of students." It is not unusual to find diametrically opposed ideas described that way.

Tool 97-Self-Assessment of Focus on Students describes specific ways you can assure that improving rigor focuses first on students.

Tool 97   Self-Assessment of Focus on Students

Strategy	Status at Our School
Are we guided by a clear vision about providing a more rigorous educational experience for students?	
How do we align staff, budget, and other resources with our vision?	
How do we use data about student learning and instructional practices to guide decision-making?	
How do we provide students and families with the resources to be successful in a more rigorous school?	
How have we involved teachers, families, and community in our effort to improve rigor?	
How do we advocate with families, community, and district personnel for support in improving rigor?	

Final Thoughts and Action Planning

The road to a more rigorous school is a journey, not an event. It won't happen overnight or by the end of the next school year. Beginning the journey is the most important step.

Once you begin, it is important to always focus on your vision of a more rigorous school. The vision is the key. Then you must link decisions about professional development, collaborative work groups, the school schedule, and the budget to make that vision come true.

Leaders have the power to transform their schools. Your vision and your commitment to working with your school community will result in a legacy that outlasts your tenure as principal. But what a wonderful legacy: a school where every child is challenged by high expectations, has all the support they need for success, and where there are multiple opportunities to demonstrate their learning.

We hope you find these tools helpful as you continue on your journey. We'd enjoy hearing from you about your experience.

My Action Plan for Moving Forward for Growth

The most important tool from this chapter in my current situation is:

_____

_____

_____

_____

_____

_____

_____

I also think the following concepts and/or tools would be useful in my situation:

_____

_____

_____

_____

_____

_____

_____

I need additional help or resources in the form of:

_____

_____

_____

_____

_____

_____

_____

My next action steps are to:

_____

_____

_____

_____

_____

_____

_____

References

Adventure Associates (2008). *Teamwork skills: Fist-to-Five Measuring Support*. Retrieved May 30, 2009, from http://www.adventureasssoc.com/resources/newsletter/nltc-fist-to-five.html.

Astuto, T. A., Clark, D. L., Read, A., McGree, K. & Fernandez, L deK P. (1993). *Challenges to dominant assumptions controlling educational reform*. Andover, MA: Regional Laboratory for the Educational Improvement of the Northeast and Islands.

Blckburn, B. (2000). *Barriers and facilitators to effective staff development: Perceptions from award-winning practitioners*. Unpublished dissertation, University of North Carolina at Greensboro, Greensboro, NC.

Blackburn, B. (2008). *Rigor is not a Four-Letter Word*. Larchmont, NY: Eye on Education.

Bower, M. (1996). *Will to manage*. New York: McGraw-Hill.

Daggett, W. (2010). *Rigor/relevance framework*. Retrieved online July 15, 2010 from http://www.leadered.com/rrr.html.

David, J. (2009). Collaborative inquiry. *Educational Leadership, 66*(4), 87–88.

DuFour, R. & Eaker, R. (1998). *Professional learning communities at work: Best practices for enhancing student achievement*. Bloomington, IN: Solution Tree.

DuFour, Ri, DuFour, Re, Eaker,R. & Many, T. (2006). *Learning by doing: A handbook for professional learning communities at work*. Bloomington, IN: Solution Tree.

Eubank, T. SREB. *Instant Credit Recovery Or Instant "Content" Recovery for Middle Grades: ICR Summary and Implementation Strategies* (unpublished whitepaper). Accessed Jan 3, 2011.

Gold, Y. & Roth. R. (1999). *The transformational helping professional: Mentoring and supervising reconsidered*. Boston: Allyn & Bacon.

Hord, S. (2009). Professional learning communities. *Journal of Staff Development, 30*(1), 40–43.

Hord, S., Rutherford, W., Hurling-Austin, L. & Hall, G. (1987). *Taking charge of change*. Alexandria, VA: Association of Supervision and Curriculum Development.

205

Hoy, W. & Tarter, C. J. (2008). *Administrators solving the problems of practice: Decision-making concepts, cases and consequences* (3rd ed.). Boston: Pearson Education.

Jolly, A. (2008). *Team to Teach: A Facilitator's Guide to Professional Learning Teams.* Oxford, OH: National Staff Development Council.

Lounsbury, J. & Johnston, J. H. (1988). *Life in the three sixth grades.* Reston, VA: National Association of Secondary School Principals.

Marx, G. (2006). *Sixteen trends: Their profound impact on our future: Implications for students, education, communities, and the whole of society.* Alexandria, VA: Educational Research Service.

Maslow, A. H. (1968). *Toward a psychology of being.* New York: John Riley.

Williamson, R. (2009). *Scheduling to improve student learning.* Westerville, OH: National Middle School Association.

Williamson, R. & Blackburn, B. (2009). *The Principalship from A to Z.* Larchmont, NY: Eye on Education.

Williamson, R. & Blackburn, B. (2010). *Rigorous Schools and Classrooms: Leading the Way.* Larchmont, NY: Eye on Education.